CARNIVAL GIRL

ISBN 13: 978-1-59955-996-4

Published by CFI, an imprint of Cedar Fort, Inc.
2373 W. 700 S., Springville, UT 84663
Distributed by Cedar Fort, Inc., www.cedarfort.com

Library of Congress Cataloging-in-Publication Data is on file

Cover design by Brian Halley
Cover design © 2012 by Lyle Mortimer
Edited and typeset by Whitney A. Lindsley

Printed in the United States of America

10 9 8 7 6 5 4 3 2 1

Printed on acid-free paper

SEARCHING FOR GOD IN THE AFTERMATH OF WAR

SONJA HERBERT

CFI
AN IMPRINT OF CEDAR FORT, INC.
SPRINGVILLE, UTAH

This book is dedicated to my amazing mother, Margot Edel, who survived the Third Reich by hiding in a circus. At 91, she is still going strong!

Many thanks also to my wonderful family. My husband, Ken, who stood by me, encouraging me through all these years, and our eleven children, who supported and loved me through all my doubts and rewrites.

CONTENTS

CONTENTS

<small>PROLOGUE</small>

MUTTI

I'M WAITING AT THE AIRPORT WITH MY HUSBAND, KEN, AND OUR two youngest daughters. My mother, whom I haven't seen for fifteen years, is arriving from Germany. In my mind, she is still the young woman who was so important to me during my childhood. I am a little girl again, excited and worried at the same time. Ignoring my teenage girls' giggles, I crane my neck to search the crowd for Mutti, as I still call her. My heart is pounding, and I'm wondering whether she made it safely. A young woman rushes through the gate, pulling her little boy, and a gaggle of teenagers greet an older couple. The overhead loudspeaker announces something unintelligible. I scan the crowds. Where is she?

Finally I see her. Her dark-blue travel suit looks freshly ironed. She marches through the gate, wheeling a large bag, as if she knows exactly where she is going. My heart swells with pride. She's smaller than I remember, but she doesn't look her eighty-four years. Her once-black hair is now an artificial auburn. The gray comes through at the roots, but her eyes are still as dark and as brilliant as ever. Mutti spies me and waves, a big smile on her face. We embrace. She doesn't speak English, so as she greets me and my husband, I translate for the grandchildren she has only seen once, when they were small.

My husband drives us home as we talk about the family in the old country. Mutti yawns. The trip must have taken its toll. While the kids bring in her luggage, she lies down for a rest in Meagan's bedroom, which

*This prologue won first prize in the December 2005 Joyous Writing Contest.

we have prepared to be hers for the length of her stay. While Mutti is upstairs getting acquainted with her room, I'm thinking about the plans we have made for this visit.

The next day, with the girls in school, Mutti and I sit down with our drinks, a cup of hot chocolate for me and a cup of instant coffee for Mutti. After a bit of prompting, Mutti begins to tell me her story.

"Before the war ended, things were terrible." She takes a sip of her coffee. "No one had any food; the Nazis were killing people indiscriminately; and everybody, hungry, cold, and afraid, was waiting for the end we thought would soon come."

* * *

My half-Jewish mother, a woman of much sorrow, despised and hated by her own government, presented the world with new life at a time when the Nazis were feeding her people by the millions to the furnaces.

During Mutti's first two pregnancies, Hitler was still in power, and Mutti didn't dare see a doctor for fear of being recognized as Jewish. My oldest sister was born in a circus caravan, far too early, and lived only a few hours.

Mutti became pregnant again early in 1945. She felt that if there were a God, maybe he finally would have mercy on her. This time, surely things would turn out all right.

In June the war ended, and Germany was again safe for people of Jewish descent. Mutti and Vati, our father, were finally able to be married by a representative of the new, thrown-together German government. Just a few weeks later, Mutti gave birth to her second baby, this time in a hospital.

Carmen too was premature. Her breathing was labored and painful, and she hardly moved. The skin on her bottom was so thin, Mutti could see the blood vessels through it.

The doctor's eyes were red with exhaustion and discouragement when he handed the new baby to Mutti. "I'm so sorry, Frau Francesco. There is nothing I can do. The incubators are destroyed, and we just don't have the resources to keep your little girl alive."

Mutti looked up, her face wet with tears. "Please, Herr Doktor, what can I do?"

"Take her home. Try to feed her. If God wills, maybe she'll survive." He smiled a tired, sad smile. "Your love can do more for her than what we can do here."

Mutti took the barely breathing baby home to their rickety, old circus caravan.

Amid putting up and taking down the circus, selling tickets, and trying to entertain the war-shocked populace, Vati and Mutti took turns feeding Carmen. She needed food every two hours, day and night. For many months, it looked like she wouldn't survive. Mutti pumped the milk for her, and they fed Carmen first by eyedropper, and then when she finally was able to suck, with a bottle.

When Carmen finally gained enough strength and started to take solid foods, diarrhea hit. For days, she screamed with cramps and lost almost all her bodily fluids. In desperation, Mutti took her to another doctor in another town, where the circus was playing at the time. This doctor was too overwhelmed with treating the wounded soldiers and civilians pouring into the western towns from the east to worry about one small baby. After a cursory examination, he told Mutti, "Your child is severely dehydrated from dysentery."

"Can you help her, please?"

The doctor shook his head. "Since she can't hold any liquids, I can't help her any more than you can. Try to keep her hydrated. That's all anyone can do for her. She might make it through."

Mutti found a pharmacy and asked what could be done for dysentery. The druggist sold her a small box with black carbon tablets. He warned her to be very careful because such medicine could easily worsen the condition. Faced with the danger of losing another child if she did nothing, Mutti ground up half of one tablet, stirred it into a bit of oatmeal, and fed it to her sick baby. Carmen survived.

* * *

Sometime in February 1947, Mutti stood, butter knife in hand, at the table in the kitchen of her circus caravan. While spreading margarine and strawberry jam on rye bread for little Carmen's breakfast, she hoped her period was just late. With unseeing eyes, she stared at Carmen, who sat on a makeshift high chair, a block of wood covered with a pillow atop a chair. The coal burning in the kitchen oven suffused the small room with warmth. Carmen stuffed small bites of bread into her jam-covered mouth. A cold, late-winter rain pounded on the thin caravan roof and ran in rivulets down the window by the kitchen table.

Mutti stood in the kitchen and watched her baby eat. She didn't know if she could do this again. So far, each of her pregnancies had produced premature babies, and Mutti was convinced she'd have another preemie if she were expecting again. She wouldn't have the energy to snatch another child from death, not with having to sell tickets in the circus and care for little Carmen.

She wiped Carmen's face, picked her up from the high chair, and placed her on her hip. Automatically, she cleaned the kitchen table, all the while thinking about her predicament. She couldn't go through this again. This time she'd break. But what else could she do?

Maybe her period was just late. She'd be all right. If this were a false alarm, she'd be very careful from now on. Mutti placed Carmen into the old playpen in the living room, sighed, and decided to tell Vati.

At noon, when Vati came in from putting up the circus tent, Mutti told him. He comforted her and told her to wait and see. If there were another baby, they would take care of it too. Surely this one wouldn't be premature, now that they had more and better food to eat. And this time they'd surely have a boy, someone to carry on the family name and the circus.

* * *

On September 29, 1947, I was born. I was lucky. I started life after the war, full-term and in great health.

On one hand, Mutti was happy. On the other hand, I wasn't the boy they wanted. They didn't even have a name for me, another girl. After taking a few days to consider the problem, Vati decided to call me Sonja, after his sister.

Eighteen months later, my sister Josefa was born. Mutti asked the doctor if there was anything she could do so she wouldn't get pregnant again, but the doctor told her there wasn't, and that she should consign herself to God's will and be glad he had given her these children.

Mutti, who lost her faith during the Nazi regime, cursed God, the doctor, and her fate. Three children were too many in these hard times. She wasn't able to care for more and would do what she could to prevent another pregnancy. But just eight months later, she was pregnant with her fourth child.

1

ABANDONED

MUTTI SITS ON THE SOFA WITH ME, A BOX OF OLD PICTURES ON the coffee table before us. She picks up a black-and-white photograph from a pile and shows it to me. "That was before you three went to the orphanage."

The picture is of Carmen, a toddler with wispy blonde hair, standing on the steps in front of the caravan. I sit on the lowest step. Josefa, still a baby at the time, isn't in the picture.

I turn the picture in my hands. "I don't remember when we took this. The first memory I have is of the orphanage."

Mutti places the photo back onto the pile by the box and turns to me, defensiveness in the turn of her mouth. "I didn't want to send you there, but I didn't have a choice. By the time the doctors discovered the kidney infection, I was more than six months along, and the baby had already kicked."

"What did the doctor say?"

"He wanted me to have an abortion. I just couldn't do it. If it meant I'd have to die, then so be it. I decided to go through with the pregnancy."

I realize how afraid she must have been, not just for us but for herself too. And she didn't have the comfort of believing in a loving God who'd be with her no matter what. Alone, she faced death, challenged fate, and gave life to yet one more child.

Had she died, we girls would have been another casualty of war. Either we would have ended up permanently in the orphanage, or we'd have gone to Communist Poland with our widowed Vati.

Mutti sits on the sofa, looking at her hands folded in her lap. "That soon after the war, food was scarce, and the nuns who ran the orphanage must have been overwhelmed with work. They didn't need three more children, and for you three it wasn't a good place to go. But we had no choice. My mother was far away in Berlin, and your Vati's family had returned to Poland. Vati couldn't work the circus and take care of all of you too." Mutti sighs. "Maybe there is a God out there somewhere, after all. Everything turned out okay. I lived through it; the baby, your brother, Franz, was all right; and you girls returned from the orphanage."

She turns to another picture, and I think of the earliest of my memories, the orphanage, where, among other things, I first learned about God and prayer.

SUMMER 1950

In the cities of a devastated Germany, groups of women cleared the bombed-out rubble of destroyed houses from the streets and sidewalks. Tired and worn out, they returned to their homes in the evenings to attend to their husbands, sons, and other male relatives, who were wounded physically and spiritually from that unjust war.

In the countryside, where Vati traveled with his small circus, fewer destroyed buildings gave testimony of the war. Vati often exchanged circus tickets for fresh food instead of buying it with the worthless German Reichsmark, the currency of that time. Still, food was scarce, war casualties abounded, and lost and abandoned children overwhelmed the orphanages.

The day we arrived at the orphanage, I was three, Carmen was five, and Josefa was eighteen months.

Vati knocked on the door, and a tall woman in black and wearing a funny black-and-white hat opened the door. She took us down a narrow hall into a large, dark room. Vati talked to her for a while, and we girls looked around. Four large windows shed a dim, rainy daylight on the cribs lining the walls. A pungent aroma, like the smell from Mutti's diaper bucket, wafted through the air.

Vati turned to us. "You be good now and mind these ladies. I'll come back for you soon." He hugged Carmen first, then me, and then picked up Josefa. I looked at Carmen. She was frowning but not crying, so I blinked at the tears threatening to spill and imitated her frown. I wasn't sure what was going on, but I'd be good, as Vati had asked. Vati handed Josefa to the woman next to him, turned, and left.

I swallowed a sob, hung on tighter to Carmen's hand, and stuck my thumb into my mouth. A baby in a crib stood on wobbly feet and hung on to the bars. Round, blank eyes stared at us. The babies wore pink and blue jumpers, to tell the boys from the girls, I thought.

The woman put Josefa down, and I held my other hand out for her.

A little girl lay in another crib. She sucked her thumb and kicked her feet. Other babies sat on potties by their cribs, looking sad. Crying filled the air. I shuddered and sucked my thumb harder. Two women hurried through the hall, one with a crying baby slung over her shoulder. Their footsteps echoed against the tiles of the floor and added a counterpoint to the wails and cries that made me wince. I wished Mutti or Vati were there. When would they return for us?

Instead of Mutti, a woman in a voluminous black dress, like a great black bird, swooped down on my sisters and me. Carmen held my hand tighter and quit twirling a strand of her blonde hair. Carmen hadn't cried when Vati left us there. Josefa held my other hand and still sobbed. Her damp blonde curls clung to her forehead. She was so little. She didn't understand.

The woman in black pulled Josefa from my side. My hand felt empty. I curled it into a fist and hugged it to my faded blue dress. From the arms of the scary woman, Josefa stared at me, her mouth a silent O. I couldn't hold back my tears any longer. Josefa screwed up her face, joined in, and stretched her arms out to me.

"Hush," the woman said. Later I learned she was a nun, and I had to address her as "Sister." She wasn't my sister, though. Carmen and Josefa were. But Vati told us to mind these women, and I wanted to be good. I called them "Sister" like they wanted.

"You're just a baby," she said to Josefa. "You belong in a crib." She carried her to an empty crib and dropped her in. Josefa pulled herself up on the bars. She stretched one hand out to me and Carmen, crying harder.

The nun turned to us. "Your sister will be all right." Her small, dark eyes darted from me to Carmen. She separated my other hand from Carmen's. "You two are bigger. You can go to the playroom."

She dragged us to a door at the far end of the room. Carmen wiped her eyes and turned to look back at Josefa. I sobbed.

The woman took us to another room, where children rocked dollies and pushed toy cars along the floor. I watched them and gradually quit crying. They seemed to be having fun. Two little boys pushed a wooden car. A girl Carmen's age rocked a dolly in her arms.

Blocks, toy cars, and old dolls littered the floor. The blocks, some plain wood and others painted bright red, yellow, and blue, looked inviting.

I looked around. No one played with the blocks, so I picked them up. They felt smooth and nice in my hand. I sat on the cool floor and put the red one on top of the blue one. Carmen took one of the dolls and inspected its clothes.

Later, a young woman wearing a cheerful pink dress came in, smiled, and took us by the hand. All the children lined up, and she led us to a room filled with tables and small chairs. Crosses hung on the walls; one of them had a sad man wearing a sort of crown on it. I wondered who that was. Carmen and I sat at one of the tables with two little boys and two other girls.

One of the nuns stood at the head of the room and told everyone to be quiet for the blessing. The children quit talking, bowed their heads, and pressed their hands together. The nun frowned at me. I looked at Carmen, who had followed the lead of the other children and bowed her head, so I did the same. Then the nun said a little poem about someone called "God" and thanked that person for the food. *That God must be a little like my Vati*, I thought, *a nice person who gives us food and things*.

After the poem, two women passed out plates with sandwiches. I was hungry and stuffed the sandwich into my mouth. The margarine smeared around my mouth, and I wiped it off with the back of my hand before I took another bite.

I finished eating and sat, watching the other children. My eyes felt heavy. A nun—I couldn't think of her as a sister—took Carmen and me to a room with beds. They looked almost like cribs with their high sides. The nun showed me to a bed. I tried to climb in but couldn't quite manage. The nun picked me up and placed me inside. Across the aisle, Carmen climbed into hers by herself.

I sat and looked across the room, searching for Josefa. I pulled myself up on the high bars encasing my bed, but I didn't find a foothold so I could climb over. I couldn't get out. I tried to squeeze out between the bars, but I couldn't push my chest and head through. I pulled back. My heart hammered, and I sobbed again. I wanted to be with Carmen.

From across the aisle, Carmen said, "Stay in. Go to sleep."

I lay down so I could see her blonde, curly hair through the slats. I sucked my thumb, and my heartbeat slowed down.

In the morning, one of the nuns took me out of the bed and made me stand in a line with the other children. I rubbed my eyes and yawned. After a while, it was my turn to go into a small room with a seat with a hole in it, just like the potty I used in our caravan, but much larger. I climbed on and peed. In another large room, I washed my hands and face in one of the porcelain bowls that stuck to the wall, not in a blue enameled washbowl like we had at home. The water flowed out of a funny-looking spout. Nobody poured it. I washed my hands and played with the running water for a moment. The nun, who was helping a little boy at the washbowl next to me, came over to me and scolded me for dawdling. "The other children are waiting," she said. "Hurry up."

* * *

Later I wandered off to see if I could find Josefa. I went to the room with the cribs and looked at the babies. Some sat or stood holding on to the bars.

I saw my sister. She sat on a potty in front of her crib, her chubby arms close to her side and her hands folded in her lap. When she saw me, she tried to get up, but a nun rushed over and pushed her back. "You haven't done your business yet," she said. "Stay on the potty."

Josefa sat back down and stretched her hands out to me. I started crying. I wanted my sister. But the nun took me by the hand and pulled me back to the playroom. I wanted to stay with Josefa, but the nun didn't want me to, and that made me feel guilty somehow.

That evening I had to go bathroom. But the nun hurried me. I just had time to pee before she pulled me off the big potty and took me back to the bedroom. She said she didn't have time to take children to the bathroom all day. I held it in.

In the middle of the night, I had to go again. I tried but couldn't get over the bars. I was afraid to call, so I lay back down. But I couldn't help it, and it came out. I closed my eyes tightly and finally fell asleep.

Rough hands woke me, pulling me from the bed. Before I could open my eyes, someone dumped me in a tub of cold water. I flailed my arms and screamed. My body shook from the icy water and my fear. "Mutti! Mutti!" I screamed. Why wasn't Mutti here? What bad thing had I done that she'd leave me here all alone?

"That's what you get when you mess your pants," the nun scolded. "You're supposed to do your business in the mornings, like the other children."

She pulled me from the water and rubbed me dry. My skin, before puckered up in goose bumps, now burned from the towel.

"You don't want to be back in diapers, do you?"

I hardly heard her through my screams.

But I remembered what she said, and in the morning I tried very hard to do both when it was my turn. A little bit came out. The next day it was even better. I wanted to be a good girl. Maybe if I were really good, Mutti would come back for me.

I must have been successful; that was the only time during our stay in the orphanage that the nuns washed me in icy water.

Many days later—though it seemed forever—Vati came to visit, so the nuns dressed us in our nice dresses. Mine was blue with yellow flowers, Carmen's was red, and Josefa's was light blue. Vati hugged us and took us outside, carrying Josefa.

During our stay in the orphanage, Josefa sat so much that I thought she forgot how to walk. But this was also because of the food we ate there, mainly cereal and no fruits and vegetables.

We walked down the sidewalk; I held Vati's hand, and Carmen held on to his jacket. Carmen asked if we could go home.

"Not yet," Vati said. "Mutti is still very sick in the hospital."

Carmen screwed up her face.

"Don't cry," Vati said. "You're a big girl. Big girls don't cry."

Carmen swallowed and stared at the ground. I looked at the burned-out ruin across the street. A few blades of grass and a yellow dandelion poked out of the rubble. The dandelion shone in the sun, like gold. I smiled and held on tighter to Vati's hand. Vati was here, we were together again, and all was well with my world. Soon we would go home to Mutti.

Vati took us to the farmers' market in town and bought each of us a banana. I turned mine over in my hands. I had never seen a banana before. He sat Josefa on a bench and showed Carmen and me how to break the top open and peel them. Then he helped Josefa eat hers. I bit into mine. It tasted wonderful, sweet and strong. I wanted another one, but Vati said one was enough. They cost too much.

After a while, Vati took us back to the orphanage. When the nun came to get her, Josefa cried and didn't let go of Vati's shirt. But he pulled her hand away and held her out to the nun.

The next time Vati came for us, we went home. Carmen gripped Vati's hand tightly and didn't let go, even when we reached the fairgrounds.

We marched around the tent on the trampled grass, avoiding a roustabout leading a horse on a rope. Behind him, I spied our white-painted caravan, curtains in the windows. It stood on its tiny rubber tires, apart from the other circus caravans lining up behind it.

From the bright sunshine outside, we entered the darker caravan. When my eyes adjusted, I glimpsed Mutti sitting on the sofa like an angel. My heart went out to her. She was so pretty; she was my Mutti. Her black hair framed her white skin, and even though she was thinner, her bosom was full and inviting. I wanted to hug her, to feel safe in her warm, motherly embrace. She leaned against the back of the sofa and held the new baby against her breast. Carmen and I ran to her, and I hugged her knees. Josefa, from Vati's arms, stretched out her hands and cried. Mutti patted my hair. I hugged her harder, unwilling to let go. She gently pulled my arms from around her legs and pushed me away to put the baby into the baby buggy by her side and take Josefa from Vati. I stared at my Mutti, my love and mainstay.

2

BRIGITTE

Mutti and I sit at the kitchen table in my house in Utah. The sun shines through the glass doors, brightening the corridor that leads to our living room. I smile at all this space and compare it to the tiny, dark caravan I lived in as a child. The first few years of my life our tiny living quarters were part of my father's circus, but I can hardly remember the animals and acrobats. Most of my memories are of traveling the carnival circuit with our small caravan, the merry-go-round, and the shooting gallery.

We're having lunch. The girls are in school, Ken is at work, and Mutti and I are ready to revisit my childhood. "I don't remember how Vati changed from being a circus owner and artist to run our carnival," I say.

"At the end of the war, we lost most of the animals because we couldn't feed them anymore." Mutti shakes her head. "We lost the circus, but we still had the horses. At first, we used them to make a living. Vati gave riding lessons in Nuremberg to the families of the American occupation forces. We received food from the Americans and went out riding together. It was a good time." She pats

SHOOTING GALLERY AND MERRY-GO-ROUND

my hand. "Child, your father was just not made to be an office worker. It would have killed him to be inside all day and work for someone else. After the Americans left, there wasn't anything else for him to do but run a carnival. The government finally printed new money and gave everybody one hundred deutschmarks, I seem to remember. For us, it was just enough to buy a used fair attraction."

"The boat attraction? That's the first one I remember."

"That's right. We even had enough money left to buy the materials to build a shooting gallery. So that's what we did."

"By that time, you had four little children. Why did your mother and stepfather never come to see us?"

Mutti takes a sip from her tea. "When I was a child, my mother beat me a lot. She used to make me sit in front of my spinach until I ate it all. I hated spinach. I finally forced it down but threw it up again, and she'd hit me and make me eat the vomit. I swore to myself I'd never hit you children. And I never did, did I?"

My eyes suddenly sting. As an adult, I have always considered my mother to be tough and pragmatic. I hadn't known about her own loveless childhood.

I reach over and pat her cool, wrinkled hand. "You never did, Mutti."

"I didn't want my mother close to you kids because she would have hit you the way she hit me when I was small. She was so impatient and harsh. Besides that, she didn't care to visit us. She hated that I lived in a carnival and not in a real apartment, like normal people." Mutti sighs. "That's all such a long time ago. I guess she did the best she could with me and your aunt Brigitte, considering the way things were then."

An incident from my early childhood pops into my mind.

"Tante Brigitte lived with us for a while, though."

Mutti nods. "Brigitte quit her apprenticeship and wanted to be in the carnival like I was. I was glad to have the help, but it didn't last very long."

"Even though I was so small, I remember what she did the day before she left."

"Brigitte was young and didn't know better. I warned her not to hit my children," Mutti says. "When she did, it was too much. We had a fight, and she went back home."

FALL 1951

Mutti put baby Franz into his buggy and turned to Carmen. "Rock him until he goes to sleep," she said and left the caravan.

The caravan seemed darker without Mutti. Carmen rocked the baby, and I watched for a while. When his eyes closed, I wandered into the kitchen. Josefa, near Tante Brigitte, sat crying on the floor. I thought she wanted Mutti, and I felt like joining her. But I was bigger, so I swallowed my tears and opened the toy drawer under the kitchen counter, pulling out a doll and hugging it.

Tante Brigitte, who was sitting at the kitchen table, ignored us. She took a knife from a drawer and started cutting slices off a loaf of bread. She put jam on one slice and placed another slice on top. My mouth watered. Strawberry jam tasted so good.

Tante Brigitte put two of the sandwiches onto a plate and left the others on the table. She looked at me. "Be good. I'll be right back." She opened the door and left, probably to take the sandwiches to Mutti in the shooting gallery and to Vati, who was running the merry-go-round.

I looked at Josefa, who had quit crying. She scrambled from the floor and stood in front of the kitchen table, stretching. She couldn't quite reach the left-behind sandwiches. I was bigger, so I dropped my doll, stood on tiptoes, and reached for the tasty food on the table.

Carmen came from the living room. "Don't do that. Tante Brigitte will be mad."

I stuck my tongue out at her. "I can do what I want. I'm big too."

I took a sandwich, broke it in half, and gave one half to Josefa.

The doll lay at my feet as I took a bite from the piece in my hand. Josefa climbed onto the kitchen bench and sat eating her half, jam smeared all over her face.

The stairs outside creaked, and the door opened. Tante Brigitte's silhouette filled the open door. She surveyed the situation in the kitchen, closed the door, and came closer, hands on her hips and a scowl on her face. "Who did this?"

I pointed to my little sister. "She's hungry,"

Even that young I knew food was scarce, and we only ate when we were allowed to. But Mutti always made sure we weren't hungry. Surely it was okay to give some food to Josefa. After all, soon it would be our turn to eat.

Brigitte reached out and, before I realized what was happening, slapped my face. I stood there, stunned. My cheek burned. I put my hand over it and cried. I had been good, hadn't I? I'd helped my sister. Maybe

I shouldn't have eaten one of the sandwich halves. Tears rolled down my cheek, and I hid my face in my hands, not understanding why I couldn't do anything right. At that moment, the door opened and Mutti came in.

She took one look at me, and her eyes grew large, her lips tightened, and she turned to Brigitte. "You don't hit my children. Don't you ever dare do that again."

I swallowed my tears, hitched a breath, and finished my sandwich with one last bite. I hadn't done anything bad. Brigitte had. I stared at her with big eyes. Adults never did anything bad, but Tante Brigitte did. Maybe not all adults were perfect.

Brigitte's eyes glistened. "Those little thieves!" She shot a murderous glance toward me. "They're spoiled, anyway. They need a good beating."

Brigitte explained that I stole a sandwich and needed to learn a lesson.

"Not that kind of lesson," Mutti said.

Brigitte's mouth was set, and her eyes flashed. "I'm leaving."

"You always leave when it's not convenient," Mutti said. "Make up your mind what you want to do. Go home and finish your apprenticeship, like I did."

Brigitte stormed from the caravan. Mutti gave a sandwich to Carmen. "What do I do now, God?" she murmured. "I need help."

I wondered who God was. Was He the same person we said little poems to in the orphanage? If so, He must be nice, but why didn't He help my Mutti?

The next day, Brigitte went back to her mother's apartment in Berlin. I was glad she was gone. She wasn't nice like my Mutti.

Now Carmen took care of us when Mutti helped in the carnival.

* * *

The stress Mutti felt must have been unbelievable, with four children under seven in a caravan, having to work and tend them at the same time. And she had no faith to sustain her.

"After Brigitte went home," Mutti tells me as we continue to talk, "I took the baby buggy with Franz with me to the shooting gallery. I wedged the buggy under the counter with the hood up, so Franz was safe. You girls stayed in the caravan next door and could see me whenever you needed to."

"I can't imagine how you managed," I say.

"It worked out all right. Except for that time when you broke open Carmen's head, we managed."

3
POWER STRUGGLES

I REMEMBER THE DAY I HIT CARMEN," I SAY. MUTTI'S REMARK ABOUT what I had done so long ago brings the memory back to me as if it had happened yesterday. "I was terrified. I was so little, only four. I didn't know what I was doing."

"I still remember," Mutti replies, taking a sip of tea from a mug sitting on the sunlit kitchen table in front of her. "You hit your sister with a glass bottle. There was blood everywhere. You were old enough to know. You did that on purpose."

"But I really didn't know."

"Sure you didn't . . ."

I quell my rising anger. Mutti, crowded and overburdened with children and the carnival, had no one to help her. When she had been a child, she had no siblings until she was eight, when her sister was born. She probably doesn't remember what it was like to be so small. But I still do.

SUMMER 1952

It was late. We ate the sandwiches Mutti made before she went to work in the shooting gallery. I wrapped my doll in an old cloth, her blanket, and put her down in a corner of the toy drawer, which I pretended was her bed.

"Sleep now," I said to my doll. "And don't cry. Mutti wants to sleep too." But the doll wouldn't quit crying. I was just about to pick her up and tell her what a bad girl she was, when Carmen slammed the toy drawer shut and told me to go to bed.

I stomped my foot. "No." Carmen was just my sister, not my mother, and she wasn't that much taller than I was either. She couldn't tell me what to do. I was big too and could do whatever I wanted when Mutti wasn't there.

Carmen grabbed my arm and dragged me through the living room into the bedroom, even though I was screaming. She shut the door after me and stayed in the living room.

I screamed harder. She couldn't do that. I was alone in the big US Army bed Carmen shared with me. If I was in bed, she should be too.

Josefa, in the smaller bed across from mine, stared at me with big, brown eyes and sucked her thumb. Through my tears, I spied an empty green wine bottle in the recycle box by Josefa's bed.

I grabbed it, pushed the bedroom door open, and screamed, "I'm big too! I don't have to do what you tell me."

Carmen reached for the bottle in my hand. "Yes, you do."

I swung it and hit her on the head.

A line of crimson snaked down from Carmen's forehead. Lips quivering, she stared at me and touched her forehead. Her hand came away smeared with red. The snake of blood reached her nose and dripped onto the floor. She ran from the caravan, screeching for Mutti.

The bottle dropped from my hands and bounced on the linoleum floor. Fear took my breath away, and I cried in terror. Had I done that? I hadn't meant to. I must be a really bad child.

Mutti rushed in with Carmen in tow. She wiped Carmen's head with a wet rag and put a bandage on it. Then she grabbed me, hard, and shook my shoulders. "You little monster! What do you think you were doing?" She dragged me to the bed and threw me down. "Don't you dare get up until tomorrow morning. You're supposed to obey your sister. Don't you ever hit her again!"

I curled up under the feather quilt and sobbed. Slowly my terror for my sister receded. Mutti had fixed what I'd done wrong.

But Mutti was right. I was a monster; I couldn't be good, no matter what. Panic rose again. Maybe Mutti and Vati would take me away, like before. This time they wouldn't come back for me at the orphanage. It would be like dying. I wasn't worthy to live with them if I couldn't be good. Shivering, with this half-realized fear burrowing into my soul, I fell asleep.

I had no comfort at that young age, just an unrealized need to be special to someone, to be loved and know I was loved. A few years later, this need would be filled in a most unusual way.

But first I had to learn about money and honesty.

4

ATTITUDES ABOUT HONESTY

UTTI AND I SIT IN A COFFEE SHOP IN DOWNTOWN SALT LAKE City. We take a break from our window-shopping and bask in the sunshine. Mutti enjoys a latte, and I have an iced chocolate.

"We couldn't afford anything like that when you were little," she says. "The locals were so tight with their money. The farmers in the small towns, where no bombs fell, had money again a few years after the war. But they didn't spend a lot at the carnival." Mutti laughs. "Sometimes, though, they forgot to take their change, and then we had a bit more."

I shudder. I realize the extent of the poverty we lived in right after the war, but even when I was very little, I hated taking money if it wasn't mine. I remember how Mutti taught me that.

SUMMER 1952

I was five. One Friday after lunch, Mutti told us to be good and mind Carmen while she left to open the shooting gallery.

Through the kitchen window, I saw Vati untie the canvas from the front of our boat ride and open the small ticket booth.

When the attractions opened and our parents worked, Carmen allowed us to leave our caravan and check out the different rides and stands, so I wandered to the ring toss that flanked our shooting gallery. Mutti waved at me and mouthed to stay close while she loaded an air gun for a customer.

As always, the candy stand attracted my attention. I wished I had a five-*pfennig* piece. I could buy licorice, hard candy, or a small piece of chocolate with it. I swallowed an imaginary bite and was about to go on, when something glinted on the trampled grass between my feet.

A coin, half hidden by a crumpled candy wrapper, sparkled in the sunshine. I bent, grabbed it, and stood up straighter. Holding my treasure made me feel like a princess, so rich. I stood in front of the candy stand, inspecting the goodies, and debated what to buy. The suckers, round and enticing on their wooden sticks, came in lemon or cherry flavors and lasted for a long time in a little girl's mouth. They and the licorice made my mouth water.

I surveyed the different pieces of chocolate. They would melt on my fingers in a sweet, gooey mess. I could suck on each one for a while. But then again, chocolate never lasted as long as the brightly colored suckers.

Finally I decided on a sucker and ran home with my treasure.

"Where did you get that?" Carmen asked.

"Let me have a lick," Josefa demanded.

"Me too!" little Franz yelled.

I held the candy away from them but eventually let them all lick it.

"I found five pfennig," I proudly declared.

My sisters went around searching the ground a long time after that, hoping to find some money too.

The next day, Mutti loaded the guns for the locals at the shooting gallery, and Vati took the tickets from the children on the swing attraction and started and stopped it. Left to myself, I got hungry when the sun sank and hoped it would be suppertime soon.

Again I wandered around outside. Many people crowded in front of the shooting gallery, and Mutti sold them shots, not seeing me. I watched a daddy buy a red sucker and hand it to the little girl next to him. How good a sucker would taste right now. Or even a sandwich. I stared at the ground for a long time but didn't find any more money.

I returned to our caravan, hoping to see my big sister making something to eat. Nobody was there. The kitchen table was bare, except for some crumbs. The hot water container, built into our kitchen range, gleamed from a stray sunbeam that entered the caravan with me. I glanced at it and spied Mutti's purse on top of the lid.

Didn't Mutti take money out of that purse when she sent Carmen to buy bread or milk from the farmers? I edged nearer and imagined what treasures that purse might hold. On my tiptoes, I stretched for the purse.

My fingers touched it, and I grabbed the handle and picked it up. It fell open. Two five-pfennig pieces dropped out, clattering on the dirty linoleum floor. I jumped and put the purse back. The two bright coins on the floor gleamed. They looked just like the one I had found on the grass. I grabbed them and stuck them into my dress pocket.

Oh, all the treasures I could buy with these coins! I stepped out into the late afternoon, hardly noticing the crowds, and squeezed between the long legs of adults. Laughter and music mingled in a familiar pattern in my ear.

At the candy stand, I surveyed the delights offered. People crowded around me. Parents bought their children treats, and older children spent their carnival money. I looked the goodies over. *Brause*, a fizzy candy, was my first choice, but I was hungry. Maybe a *Mohrenkopf*, a sweet, marshmallowy confection covered with chocolate? I picked out two pieces of chocolate, which were five pfennig each. I peeled them as I walked from the stand and stuffed them into my mouth.

When I returned from my adventure, Mutti was making sandwiches in the kitchen. Since, in my mind, Mutti knew everything, I was sure she also knew about me taking the money. But she didn't yell at me, so it was probably okay to take money.

The next day, again alone in the kitchen, I looked for Mutti's purse. I found it on the counter opposite the kitchen table. I fumbled with the snap and the purse opened, but as I groped inside, I heard a creak. Someone came up the steps outside the caravan. I jumped, and the purse fell from my fingers just as Mutti opened the door. She pushed me out of the way and snatched the purse from the floor. "What do you think you're doing? I work myself to exhaustion so you don't have to go hungry, and here you are, stealing from me!"

She pulled me by my ear and dragged me through the living room. My ear burned from her tight pinch, and I whimpered, trying to suppress my tears.

"If I can't trust you, you little thief, you can't go outside. Stay in bed until I allow you to get up."

She pushed me into the bedroom. I climbed onto my bunk, my face wet with tears, and burrowed into my feather quilt. I hadn't known it was wrong to take money. Now I understood, and I'd never do it again.

Mutti woke me and made me join the family for sandwiches. While we ate, she told the others what I had done. Carmen and Josefa called me "thief," and I yelled at them and kicked my feet.

"I'm not a thief!"

Why wouldn't they leave me alone? It didn't matter what I did, it always was wrong. I didn't want to be a thief. I wanted to be good and have Mutti love me.

Mutti said, "You're giving me a headache. You're such a loudmouth."

"Loudmouth! Loudmouth!" my sisters yelled. Little Franz joined in. I held my hands to my ears. I wanted to scream as loud as I could so they would hear me and leave me alone, but Mutti already berated me for being loud. I pressed my lips together and cried quietly.

* * *

I finish the last of my iced chocolate and look at Mutti. Strange she never realized what a mixed message she gave us children so long ago. But I did learn from it, and I have lived an honest life.

I smile. "We really needed the money right after the war," I say. "I had it a lot easier with my kids."

"Your father and I couldn't afford such luxuries as an ice cream or a cold drink for years," Mutti says. She finishes her drink and gets up. "Let's go."

5
WHAT'S IN A NAME?

Mutti and I decide to stay home on Tuesday to reminisce. We sit at the kitchen table, drinking our respective coffee and hot chocolate and looking at old pictures. Outside the sliding-glass doors, the early morning sunshine lights up the few dandelions in the lawn so they look like drops of gold.

Mutti shuffles through the pictures and pulls out an old black-and-white, postcard-sized photo. On it, like the pipes on a calliope, the four of us children line up in order of height in front of our caravan.

LIKE PIPES ON A CALLIOPE

She points to me, the second in the row. "You were such a pretty baby."

I hadn't known she thought I was pretty. I wish she had told me. I scrutinize myself in the photo. I'm wedged between Carmen and Josefa. My brother, Franz, the youngest at about two, stands on the other side of Josefa. I see myself, a five-year-old, wearing a light dress with small flowers and knee socks that have slipped down on my ankle-high shoes. My hair is cropped close to my ears, and I squint in the sun. I hold a Shasta daisy.

*This chapter received an honorable mention in the January 2006 Laughing Gull Writing Contest

Mutti says, "We used to call you Rosebud, because you have such pretty lips. And you loved flowers so much."

I stare at the photo. Yes, I recollect loving flowers and picking them whenever I could. But when did Mutti call me Rosebud? That must have been when I was a baby.

* * *

Mutti had nicknames for everyone in the family. Sometimes she used them as endearments, but more often to express dissatisfaction.

Vati she called *Pilzchen* when she was happy with him, and *Giftpilz* when she wasn't. I don't know why she picked those names, which mean "little mushroom," and "toadstool."

I can still hear Mutti call through the open caravan door, *"Pilzchen, essen kommen* [Come, eat]."

Vati would put down the boards he screwed together for our shooting gallery or lean a section of merry-go-round fence against the pack trailer, where he stowed the disassembled attractions while we were traveling. He'd stub out his cigarette, wipe his sweaty brow with the back of his hand, and come up the rickety four caravan steps for lunch.

Mutti called Carmen *Schnecke* [snail] because she was so little and slow. When Mutti used the diminutive *"Schneckchen"* [little snail], she was happy with her.

When I was about four or five, Mutti started calling me *Klappe* [big mouth] because I talked so much and cried easily. A few years later, I acquired a second name, *die Dumme* [the dummy]. When I didn't understand something, when I asked for clarification, or when I wondered how something fit together, Mutti called me dummy.

After I lost sight in my right eye, I lost my depth perception, but I didn't know it, and Mutti probably didn't either. Little accidents multiplied, and every time I broke, spilled, or dropped something, Mutti called me dummy. Soon my siblings followed suit, making me feel even more incompetent.

When she felt good about me or I pleased her, she called me *"Sonnenscheinchen"* [little sunshine]. When I heard this, it was as if the sun rose in my heart.

* * *

Now, sitting at the table, Mutti smiles. "It was hard," she says, "but we did have fun. Do you remember who *Grashüpfer* was?"

"I remember," I say.

* * *

Soon after Mutti had Franz, someone gave her a pretty green dress with small, black polka dots. The dress fit Josefa perfectly, and she loved it. She went outside on the grass and danced under the clouds, the swing ride and the shooting gallery framing her. After a few moments, turning in circles and singing was too slow for her, and she quit dancing and started jumping.

Mutti sat on the stairs in front of the open caravan door. Franz nuzzled in the crook of her arm while she watched Josefa. She laughed.

"Josefa is a real *Grashüpfer* [grasshopper] in her green dress," she said. The name stuck until Josefa was a teenager.

Mutti also had names she called all of us when she was angry or frustrated, none of them positive. When Josefa was learning to read in first grade, she had some trouble. Many afternoons after school, Mutti tried to teach her to read, but Josefa could never please her. I sat in the kitchen, still as a mouse with a book in front of me, trying to shut out Mutti's loud berating.

"You ungrateful brat," Mutti's voice would come from the living room. "Don't carry on so and make my life miserable. Read!" She wrung her hands.

Josefa screwed her eyes shut and cried harder.

Mutti insisted. She pointed to a letter. "What is that one? Huh? Speak up, will you?"

Josefa whispered something.

Mutti jumped from the sofa, folded her hands, and looked heavenward. "What did I do to deserve such selfish wretches?" she said and stormed off.

When Josefa got older, she finally learned to read. Then Mutti began to comment on how beautiful she was and how she looked so much like Mutti when she had been young.

Carmen and I were jealous of the attention our younger sister got from Mutti, and soon we called Josefa Beauty as a term of disparagement. We called her Beauty when we wanted to let her know that we thought she was stuck up, and not all that beautiful anyway.

Mutti and Vati called my brother Franz "centimeter" when he was little. We girls had no idea what that meant until much later.

* * *

Now, sitting at the table and looking at the pictures, Mutti tells me the story.

"After three daughters, your father gave up on a son," she begins. "When Franz was born and the doctor announced we had a boy, your father stared at me in amazement, mouth open.

"'He looks just like the other babies,' I said.

"'But he's different,' Vati said. 'He's my son!'

"I looked at the baby, looked at your father, and said, 'All that fuss for about one extra centimeter. That's all the difference between him and a girl.' Vati started laughing, and the name stuck. We called Franz 'centimeter' from then on."

When Franz was older and went to school with us girls, Vati made him help with the merry-go-round more and more. On many summer days, when the door to our caravan was open to let the sunshine in, I watched Vati and Franz work together putting up or taking down the shooting gallery and merry-go-round. One day, Franz brought a picture for the merry-go-round from the pack trailer. Four thick, blue-painted wooden slats framed the large canvas. Franz couldn't quite carry the picture, and he struggled to keep it from dragging on the trampled grass of the fairground. His blond head peeked a few centimeters over the grinning face of Mickey Mouse on the picture.

Vati tightened a picture of Donald Duck in the center of the merry-go-round and looked around. "Hurry up," he said. "You're so slow, like a liverwurst. Can't you do something fast for once, like other people? Come on, liverwurst."

VATI AND FRANZ

We never knew why Vati called Franz liverwurst, but the rest of us called him that too, and it was never a term of endearment.

* * *

"We had a little more money by the time Eva was born," Mutti now says. "Eva was such a happy child."

Mutti called my youngest sister *kleiner Frosch* [little frog].

I look at a picture that had appeared in a newspaper in 1957. It shows the shooting gallery with Carmen, twelve years old, inside. Josefa, Eva, and I stand outside. Josefa leans against the counter, talking to Carmen, and I stand next to her, tightly holding on to little Eva's hand. Three-year-old Eva, her blonde curls in disarray, looks up at me. The title over the newspaper picture is "Carnival Children."

Eva was alone a lot. During the carnival season, when our business was open, Carmen helped in the shooting gallery. I was a ticket taker on the merry-go-round, and Josefa cooked and ran errands.

Franz, as the only boy, helped Vati run the merry-go-round, and Eva was often left to her own devices.

* * *

Now Mutti puts down the newspaper picture. "We did have some good times, didn't we, child?" she asks.

I pat her hand. She's so small. "Yes," I say. "We did."

6

WINTER QUARTERS

WE STEP FROM THE HOUSE INTO THE BRIGHT SUMMER SUNSHINE. Mutti squints. "I left my sunglasses on the table."

"I'll get them for you." I dash back into the house.

When I bring them out, Mutti says, "You sure have nice weather here. I bet your winters are really nice too."

"It can get cold here. And we get a lot of snow, much more than we get in Germany. But I remember when we stayed in Atzbach. That was a terrible winter."

"It sure was. I'm glad it doesn't get that cold very often in Germany."

A warm breeze caresses us as we walk toward the nearby mall, and my mind flashes back to that winter in Atzbach.

WINTER 1953–54

We didn't travel in the winters. It would have been too cold for the locals to frequent our attractions. Usually by November, Vati found a town or city willing to harbor our caravan.

After we safely settled into our winter quarters, Vati fixed and improved the caravan and the attractions. He mended torn canvas, painted new pictures for the merry-go-round, and repainted the shooting gallery.

Eva, my youngest sister, was born in winter quarters in the early spring of 1955, right before we started traveling again.

The year before, the winter of 1953–54, was the first time I remember winter quarters. That fall, our caravan settled under the vast roof of the threshing floor in Atzbach, a small town in central Germany.

Our caravan consisted of the caravan, the pack caravan, our tractor, and Vati's motorcycle. Everything was huddled in a semicircle on the concrete of the roofed-over place where the farmers threshed their wheat after the harvest.

The large roof of the threshing floor, held up by thick wooden beams spaced widely along the sides and in the center, protected our small caravan that winter. The village lay about one kilometer away, a narrow dirt road our only connection with the town.

Mutti walked with us on our first day of school. We marched along a small, marshy pond and a copse of trees, maneuvering the damp, weedy ruts that led to town.

Soon we came to the paved road and found a narrow sidewalk to walk on. Toward the center of town, a large building dominated the smaller shops around it.

"That's your school," Mutti said. She steered us toward the building.

I looked up and stopped short, pulling on Mutti's hand. "What's that?" I said and pointed at the roof of the school building.

A large clump of sticks, almost twice as wide as the chimney it sat on, was perched haphazardly on top of the roof.

Carmen took my lead and pointed too. "Look," she said. "It looks like a humongous nest."

"It *is* a nest," Mutti replied. "Come on, it's getting late."

Still craning my neck to see the nest, I almost ran into a lamppost.

Mutti dragged Carmen and me into the school. A cluster of little boys squeezed by, and bigger girls stopped to stare at us. Mutti ignored them and found the principal's office, where she introduced us. Then she took us to our different classrooms and left. That day, during school, all I thought about was the nest. I wondered what the birds who built the big nest looked like.

The nest was one of the first things I learned about at Albert Schweitzer School. The teacher told us it was a stork nest. In the winters, it was empty, but every spring the same stork couple came back to Atzbach. They would live in their nest and raise their little storks there. In the fall, they would leave again for a warmer climate, maybe Spain or Africa.

The fact that the storks were a real family delighted me. They took care of their children, and they traveled, just like we did. The more I heard about them, the more I wanted to see them. I admired the pictures the teacher showed, and I couldn't wait for spring and for them to arrive. I hoped Vati wouldn't make us leave before they came back.

* * *

As time passed, snow fell, and soon deep snowdrifts covered the rutted path to the school.

I had to walk home alone sometimes because Carmen's class let out later. When Carmen was with me, it wasn't so bad, but I dreaded going home alone.

First, surrounded by the village children on their way home, I marched along the *Bürgersteig* [sidewalk] to the end of town. That was fun, because the local burghers kept the sidewalk free of snow. I meandered along, admiring the brown-and-white patterns on the old houses with their cheery green shutters. For the first time in my life, I wondered what it would be like to live in a house and not travel. I was sure it would be warmer than the caravan.

One by one, the town children disappeared from the sidewalk into different houses and buildings. Women in thick winter coats passed me by, holding their small, green or red crocheted shopping bags, their heads covered with woolen scarves.

Cars hobbled along the cobblestones on the side streets until they came to the main street, where smooth asphalt greeted them.

When the sidewalk ended, I balled my fists, took a deep breath, and turned into the rutted path leading to the threshing floor and our caravan. Deep snow covered the ruts most of that winter, such that I couldn't always tell where they were. I stumbled through the snow, occasionally misjudging and falling into the deep drifts over the ruts. When I started shivering and couldn't feel my feet anymore, I stuffed my mittened hands into my pockets and stomped my way through the snow a little faster.

One freezing day, I trudged through thick, white drifts, fighting my way with every step while the wind blew the snow around my cold legs. I had to pee. The way was so long and I was so cold that finally, almost without my noticing it, I wet my pants. I felt like crying, but I was too big to do that. At least my legs felt warm for a moment, but then I became really cold as I fought my way home.

A chorus of "Shut the door" and a burst of warmth greeted me when I pushed away the blanket Vati had nailed in front of the door to keep the heat in and the cold drafts out.

I hung my coat up on the hook by the door and stood as close to the potbellied stove in the living room as I could. I hoped my wet underpants and stockings would dry quickly and that Mutti wouldn't notice that they were wetter than they usually got from the snow. After all, I was already in school, and Carmen and Josefa would make such fun of me if they found out. And I was sure Mutti would be mad.

Nobody noticed, to my relief.

When the wan daylight deepened, Mutti switched on the electricity. After I did my homework and had a piece of buttered bread and hot cocoa for supper, I went to bed in the back compartment, our bedroom.

Our bedroom didn't have heat. A wooden door that was almost always closed separated it from the rest of the caravan. Mutti said we didn't need a warm bedroom, since we had nice, warm feather ticks to sleep under.

Early in the mornings, when Carmen and I woke to get ready for school, I lay under my feather tick for just another minute, admiring the frost flowers on the brown painted walls. They looked like fine white paintings, each one different but all symmetrical and pretty enough for a princess. *If I were a princess*, I thought, *I would live in town, in a white house with brown beams crisscrossing the outside and nice green shutters. I'd have flowers in my window boxes that would look just like my frost flowers.*

I finally rose and, with goose bumps already forming on my bare arms, slipped on my undershirt. It had two strips of extra cloth sewn to it, going from the shoulders over my chest to the bottom of the shirt, where they ended in garters. I pulled on my warm, knitted stockings and fastened them with the garters, then slipped a dress over my head, put on my warmest knitted sweater, and buttoned it up.

Carmen and I hurried into the living room, where the sofa was still pulled out, with Mutti and Vati on it, covered up with their feather tick. It was a bit warmer in the living room, since last night's coal in the potbellied stove still had heat.

Vati got up and restarted the fire in the stove. Carmen and I roasted slices of rye bread on the stove and spread them with jam and sometimes with a bit of margarine. After we ate this breakfast, we bundled up in our coats and left for the long walk to school.

* * *

By Christmas, I knew all the letters and could sound them out. I told everybody I could read, but what I sounded out still didn't make sense to me.

All I remember about my presents that Christmas is my plate with cookies and a book, a real book.

In our small caravan, we had no room for books. Mutti liked to read, so she went to the local lending libraries and borrowed books for five pfennig each.

That Christmas Eve, I sat on the edge of the sofa in the living room, close to the wood stove and the heat it produced. I sounded out the words on the pages of my brand-new book and was so surprised when suddenly the sounds made sense, and I understood what I was reading! It was exhilarating. I went to bed that night hugging my book to my chest the way my little sister hugged her dolly.

After that, in spite of the weather, the way to and back from school was almost worth it. The teacher never yelled at me and smiled when I read out loud in class. And sometimes he let me borrow books to take home. When I got to take a book home, I sat on the kitchen bench and read while Josefa and Franz played on the living room floor with wooden blocks left over from Vati's work.

* * *

One day in early spring, the teacher said, "Children, close your books. Let's line up to go outside."

We lined up two-by-two. I rose and found my line-up partner, a large girl with braids, named Martha. She was nice. She sometimes let me join when she and her friends played hopscotch or catch during recess.

Whispers buzzed around the room. Since I had been immersed in the story we had been reading in turns, I hadn't heard a fire alarm or anything like it. So I thought maybe we had a fire drill, which was why we had to go outside.

Holding Martha's hand, I followed the teacher into the yard. I shivered in the chilly air and wrapped my coat tighter around me. The teacher pointed to the chimney. "Look up, class. What do you see?"

I squinted at the rooftops and knew right away what the teacher meant. In chorus with the rest of the class, I called, "The storks!"

Two large shadows over the nest had clarified into big birds with long necks and pointed beaks. Their wings looked almost like umbrellas, they were so wide. The storks flew around their nest with slow, steady movements. Their sticklike legs extended and their black-and-white wings slowly folding against their big bodies, they glided into the nest on the chimney, surprisingly graceful for such large birds. One of them held a small, wiggling animal in its beak. It pointed its beak toward the sky and opened it, and the wriggling thing, which was probably a frog, disappeared into it.

I felt sorry for the frog, but I forgot about it in my delight at finally seeing the storks. The storks had arrived, and my family was still here! Now they would lay eggs and then have babies. I probably wouldn't be here when the babies arrived, but that didn't dampen my happiness. I clapped my hands and jumped, laughing. When we had to return to the classroom, I dragged my feet until Martha pulled at me and said, "Come already. They're just dumb storks. You can look at them again when school is out."

On a sunny but chilly day, a few days before we moved on again, the teacher took us on a field trip into the swampland at the edge of town. With my coat buttoned, I marched after the other children through the wet grasses. I hardly noticed the cold or the wetness of the damp grass soaking through my stockings. Instead, I scanned the edge of the open water for the storks while the teacher pointed out the different kinds of animals that storks ate.

Two big shadows separated from the horizon, and the storks landed about a quarter of a kilometer away from us. I laughed when I saw them walk. They looked like tall, fussy people who stepped into the cow dung that often dotted the village roads in the summers.

At the water's edge, one of the storks speared its beak into the water. I exclaimed in delight when it pulled out its beak, holding a hapless, wriggling fish.

When we finally said good-bye on our last day of school in Atzbach, I was sad to leave the storks and the nice teacher. I didn't know that the next summer I would experience something even more profound than the storks, something that would change my life forever.

7

HIS HEALING HANDS

KEN AND I TAKE MUTTI TO THE DEMOLITION DERBY AT THE San-pete County Fair.

Mutti shades her eyes from the setting sun's glare and takes in the line of old Chevys, Fords, and Dodges with their red, green, and blue splashes of paint and large numbers on their sides. She smiles, excitement bright in her eyes. "We don't have demolition derbies in Germany."

I watch her sit on the edge of the bench, pointing out her favorite, a black sedan with painted-on flames.

"*Schneller!* [Go faster!]" she yells with a big grin on her face. Finally, when only one of the cars still moves, the show is over. We get up and work our way through the throngs and the smell of gasoline and sawdust.

Mutti says, "These guys are like the carnival people. They make the rounds all through the state, riding those cars professionally. I know how that works."

I slow my pace. "I don't think that's right. As far as I know, they're locals who have fixed up a car especially for the derby."

Mutti smiles. "They're professionals. You're so unworldly."

"Don't say that, Mutti. I've done well so far in my life. I'm not as naïve as you think."

"Even as a child you were too trusting. Always believed what other people told you. I still remember how you used to go to church in those little villages. As if they told the pure truth. You believed it all."

I'm quiet, working on subduing a sudden rush of old conflicting feelings. Like so long ago when I was small, I want to please Mutti, to make her understand me, but I realize I will never be able to explain to her what happened to me one summer night when I was almost eight.

SUMMER 1955

Carmen, Josefa, and I marched home from the school we attended that week. Carmen slowed and put a lock of her blonde hair behind her ear. "I learned about Jesus today," she declared.

"Who's Jesus?" I asked.

"He's the Son of God," Carmen said. "He loves everybody, especially children."

"Does he love them even when they are bad?"

"Yes. The teacher said you can go to Jesus with all your problems. He'll always love and help you."

"Where is Jesus?" Josefa asked.

"He's in heaven. You can't see him, but he sees you."

"Then how can you go to him?" I asked.

"You can pray. You fold your hands, so." Carmen stopped, shrugged to settle the satchel on her back, and pressed her palms together in front of her chest. "You hold your hands like that, then you thank him for everything and tell him all your troubles."

That sounded great to me. I needed someone to talk to, and Jesus was just right. He seemed a lot like my father, except maybe he would stop whatever he did in heaven and listen to me. My Vati was always too busy to listen to me, or he would just play with Franz. Jesus probably also didn't mind that I was a girl, not a boy. I decided to pray that night in the bed I shared with Carmen.

By the time I went to bed, however, I had forgotten about it.

* * *

A few weeks later, I played in the dirt between our caravan and the tractor while Vati put up the merry-go-round on the fairgrounds of yet another town. A local girl in a dress with large pockets came up to me, smiling shyly. "Can I climb the tractor?"

"No, my father doesn't like it when we play on it." I noticed some papers peeking from her dress pocket. I pointed at them. "What is that?"

She pulled out three small booklets and showed them to me.

I looked them over. They had pictures and didn't seem too hard to read. A kindly looking man with a beard smiled at me from the first page.

The girl pointed to the picture. "That's Jesus."

"Jesus," I repeated. He looked nice. I remembered I had planned to pray. Maybe Jesus hates me now. But Carmen had told me he loves all children, even when they are bad. I looked from the booklet to the girl. "He's in heaven and loves us, right?"

She nodded. "It's what my pastor says." She held the pamphlets out to me. "You can have them. I can get more from my church."

I thanked her and stuffed them into my pocket to read later.

In the evenings, we children usually sat around the kitchen table and played quietly. Mutti and Vati listened to the radio, read, or played chess in the middle compartment of the caravan. If we were quiet, they sometimes forgot we weren't in bed yet and let us stay up longer.

That night, I pulled the pamphlets from my pocket to read. One story told about a girl who cried because she lost the money her mother had given her to buy bread. The girl remembered that Jesus would help, so she stood in a corner and prayed. When she looked around after the prayer, she found her money.

I really liked that story and the others like it. At the end of each story, it said to be as good as you could, and Jesus would always love and protect you.

When I went to bed that night, I sat up and folded my hands the way Carmen had shown me. In the bunk beds on the other side of the narrow aisle, Franz and Josefa, fast asleep, made little bumps under their feather quilts. Carmen wasn't in bed yet.

I whispered, "Dear Jesus, I love you. I read about you, and I'm glad you love me. I will try to be really good from now on, so you can be proud of me." I snuggled into my feather quilt. The warmth enveloped me, hugging and protecting me. I went to sleep feeling safe and happy.

THE FAMILY 1955

In the morning, when Mutti spread margarine on our breakfast rolls, I bowed my head, folded my hands, and started to thank Jesus for the food.

Carmen stared at me. "What are you doing?"

"I'm praying."

Mutti shook her head

in disapproval. "Praying won't do you any good, ever," she said, her black eyes hard and cold. "You're so naïve."

I looked at my roll. My stomach clenched, and I wasn't hungry anymore. Mutti and my sisters thought I was stupid. But I wasn't! They didn't understand about Jesus, and that he loved me. I had prayed to him last night, and I was sure he had listened. If Mutti could just understand, she'd be proud of me.

I didn't want my family to think I was stupid, so I decided I would never pray in public. However, after that, I seldom forgot my quiet prayers in bed.

* * *

One night, I woke up shaking. I had another nightmare. In my dream, I saw dead bodies and skeletons under our caravan, ready to grasp my ankles and pull me under. I suppressed a whimper. Mutti, who slept with Vati on the living room sofa, might hear me and get mad. She hated it when one of the children woke her up in the middle of the night.

In my mind I saw the skeletons reaching out for me. I slid under the covers, trying to still the shivers coursing through my body, but instead of relaxing, I tensed up even more, curling into a tight ball and hugging myself. I couldn't get the dream out of my mind. If Mutti couldn't help, I thought, maybe God could. Still hiding under the feather quilt, I straightened enough to fold my hands and ask Jesus to make the skeletons and bad dreams go away. I ended my prayer with "amen," and almost immediately a glow of warmth and safety coursed through me. I straightened out and pulled the quilt away from my head so I could breathe better. Eyes wide open, I stared into the pitch dark. I looked straight up and became aware of a bright, shiny light above me, which solidified into a golden hand over my head. The hand descended until it almost touched my face. An amazing, soothing feeling of being loved and accepted flowed through me from my scalp to my toes. A deep peace washed over me. I knew without a doubt that God was aware of me, knew me, loved me, and would never leave me.

* * *

Vati made a right turn and pulled the caravan to the center of the little town where we would hold our carnival in the marketplace. The caravan stopped swaying, and the steady *chug, chug* of the tractor quit. A bump on the front door told me Vati had connected the stairs. A moment later, Mutti rushed in from guiding the car. We girls unlocked the closets, and Mutti inspected the china to make sure it had survived once more. As soon as Mutti declared everything was all right, she would start supper, and we children burst from the caravan.

I stood in a warm breeze and checked out the marketplace. Across the street, a large old church dominated the houses around it. It was built of heavy, gray stone, interspersed with round and oval windows of many-colored glass. This is God's house, I thought. I loved these old stone churches, with their tall spires pointing toward heaven, and the bells on Sunday mornings. They sounded so peaceful, ringing in a new Sunday. I walked across the fairgrounds and the cobblestone street and stood in front of the large wooden doors, not daring to open them.

An old woman, bundled in her coat in spite of the warm spring weather, pushed by me and pulled the door open. She turned, looked at me, and said, "You can come in too. Just be quiet."

I followed after her. The woman stopped by a small stone bowl and dipped her fingers into the water. I wondered if I should do that too. I didn't know what it meant, so I didn't. The woman walked down a dark aisle and knelt between two benches.

I looked up and forgot about the woman. The large arched windows let in muted light in red, green, royal blue, and other colors. Splotches of pink and green draped across the stone floor and onto the pews. One window showed a glass picture of a beautiful woman with a baby in her arms, dressed in red and blue flowing clothes. A bright yellow ring circled her golden hair. The sun shone through the image and made her look as if she radiated holiness, mercy, and love. Her eyes were blue, not dark like my mother's. I smiled at her. I knew she was Mary, the Mother of Jesus. On the other windows, images of old people with yellow circles around their heads caught my attention. They held books or staffs.

I walked down the aisle and sat on one of the benches, admiring the windows. Straight ahead was an image of Jesus on a cross, the crown of thorns on his bent head. Red blood seeped down his forehead.

Poor Jesus! I promised him that I would always love him and I would try not to add to his pain with my sins.

After a while, I walked home with a smile. I had finally seen the inside of a church, and I liked it. The peaceful, quiet vastness seemed the perfect place for Jesus, and the beauty of those amazing colored windows impressed my heart with astonishment and delight. Jesus, who loved me, lived in such a wonderful place.

In school the next morning, one of the girls came up to me at recess. "When does the carnival start?"

"My Vati opens the merry-go-round early in the morning on Saturday. On Sundays we start when church is over."

"I have to go to Sunday morning Mass with my brother, even though it's fair time. But I'll come right after lunch. I can't wait!"

Suddenly I had an idea. "When does Mass start?" I asked. "Can I go with you?" I blurted it out before I could change my mind.

"Sure. Look for me in front of the church at nine."

Sunday morning I wolfed down my breakfast roll and glass of milk. Mutti was making coffee.

"I'm going to that church," I announced. "I want to know what it's like."

"Go ahead," Mutti said. "That will get you out of my hair for a while. But come right back when they are finished, hear?" Mutti looked at my sisters. "Do any of you want to go with her?"

Carmen giggled. Josefa shook her head.

I hurried out and ran across the street, where the girl from school waited with her little brother in tow. I sat next to her on one of the benches in the back, and she showed me what to do during the service. I learned when to kneel, how to make the sign of the cross, and even some of the chants. My knees on the hard kneeler, I watched the priest in front of the crucifix, repeated the prayers as best I could, and felt that Jesus smiled down on me—the real Jesus in heaven, not the sad one on the cross in this church.

After that, if the church wasn't too far from our carnival place, I went to Mass or if I happened to find a Lutheran church, to their Sunday services. Mutti would let me go to have me out of the caravan for a bit and to have some peace and quiet. I usually asked around at school, and when I found a child who let me tag along, I went with her.

After my vision, Heavenly Father was never far from me. I turned to him for help and succor, even that time when Tschilper had to die.

8

TSCHILPER

MUTTI COMES FROM MEAGAN'S ROOM.

"Your cat wandered into my room last night," she says, shuddering. "I don't like cats."

"I remember." Long-forgotten disappointment surfaces. "When one of the town children wanted to give me a kitten, you didn't let me have it."

"There was no room in the caravan. Besides, we did have pets, didn't we?"

Yes, we had pets. Two of them. Even though I was still very small at the time, I clearly remember the first pet we had. In her struggle to feed and clothe all of us, Mutti had gotten an addition to our food supply, but it turned into our first pet. It all started in 1955, when I was going on eight.

1955

I sat on the steps of our caravan, a reading primer on my lap. The late-spring sun shone on the trampled grass of the fairgrounds. Vati lugged another one of the large pictures sporting Disney characters from the open pack trailer toward our half-erected merry-go-round. Mickey Mouse grinned at me from the picture, and I wished I had a comic book I could look at instead of the boring reading homework the teacher in this town assigned. I returned to the primer and was reading another sentence when a shadow fell on my book.

*This chapter was a finalist in the M Review Writing Contest

I looked up. A man in a mail carrier's uniform stood in front of the caravan's steps. He looked at me with eyes embedded in a net of wrinkles. I squinted at him. He placed a large box on the grass and stretched. Soft tweeting noises came from several small holes punched in the box.

"Is this where Margot Francesco lives?" the mailman asked.

I nodded. "She's my mother."

"This box is for her, then."

I rose, hurried up the steps, and pulled the door open.

"Mutti, the mailman has a box for you."

Mutti dropped the spoon in her hand onto the kitchen table and pushed me aside. When she saw the box, her dark eyes lit up. She carried it to the kitchen table, where she inspected it, smiling.

Josefa crowded beside me and stood on her toes, trying to see. Franz climbed onto the converted bus seat by the kitchen table and reached for the box.

Mutti moved it out of his reach. "Here they are," she said. "Soon we'll have eggs any time we want them, nice and fresh."

She carefully cut the lid open with a knife. Inside, buffered by shredded newspaper, eight tiny, yellow chicks ambled around, bumping into each other. Thin cheeping sounds floated from their small, orange beaks.

"Can we play with them?" Josefa asked.

"No. When they grow up, they'll lay eggs. Then you can eat as many as you want."

Josefa frowned at the chicks. "That's a long time."

That evening Mutti encased the box with feather pillows and left it on the kitchen table.

That night I lay in my bunk bed thinking about the little chicks. I hoped they wouldn't be lonely. When I finally fell asleep, I dreamed of chicks toddling around in the kitchen, looking for their Mutti.

The next morning, when Mutti took the pillows and the lid off the chickens' box, one of them lay cold and stiff, its little feet sticking straight up. Mutti poked it with a pencil and pronounced it dead.

I went to school disappointed and sad. By the time I returned home, six chicks were left, and eventually all died, except for one.

The fluffy, yellow survivor made cheeping sounds as it shambled around in its box.

Vati declared that this chicken needed a name.

"Why not call it Tschilper?" Carmen suggested.

Gleefully, my sisters and I copied the sound the little chicken made. "Tschilp, tschilp," we imitated.

Little Franz too piped in and mimicked the chicken's sounds.

But Mutti's face was fierce. "We will not name that chicken," she declared. "I want it to contribute to our food supply, not be a pet."

Vati stubbed out his cigarette and grinned. "Tschilper it is, then," he said.

Mutti huffed, her mouth a thin line of disapproval, but she didn't protest. At that moment, our little chicken became a pet in everybody's eyes, except Mutti's.

One day, with our caravan parked in another small-town marketplace, I watched Mutti and Vati at breakfast.

"Tschilper is no chicken," Vati declared.

I forgot to eat. No chicken? What else could it be? Maybe it was a duck?

"It's too . . . Just wait and see," Mutti said. Her voice was tight and strained, and she wasn't smiling.

Vati laughed, patted Mutti's back, and left to open the shooting gallery for business.

For days I wondered what Vati meant, until Carmen told me, "Tschilper can be our pet now. He'll never lay eggs because . . . he's a boy."

"What do you mean, a boy?" I asked.

"He's a boy chicken, silly. A rooster."

She was right. Tschilper eventually developed into a gorgeous green, brown, and black Bantam rooster with a lovely orange crest and wattle, and Mutti never did get her eggs.

But she didn't give up. One morning young Tschilper, still in his box for the night, crowed at the break of dawn.

I woke, slipped out of bed, and wandered into the living room, where Mutti and Vati slept on the pull-out sofa.

Mutti climbed out from under the feather quilt and picked up Tschilper out of his box. She went through the kitchen with the rooster under her arm, threw him out the door, and returned.

"That darned bird," she muttered. "We should eat it."

I stared at her, biting my lip. Surely she wasn't serious. It wasn't so bad that Tschilper made noise. I was often noisy too, and she would never eat me. But a deep frown creased her forehead under her disheveled black hair. She rubbed her eyes, saw me, and shooed me back to bed.

After that, Tschilper stayed outside, except when we traveled. While Vati pulled our caravan with his old tractor from one town to the next, Tschilper stayed in his box, his head under his feathers, and made sleepy sounds. When we weren't traveling, he roosted on the axles between the wheels of our caravan.

Mutti had a bag of chicken feed. I followed her one morning as she went out, took a handful, and strewed it onto the ground.

She made clucking noises, and when Tschilper ran out from under the caravan, her face softened and she smiled. "Here's your breakfast, you crazy bird," she said.

Tschilper looked up from pecking at the kernels and made a soft half-crowing sound. I thought it was his way of saying, "Thank you."

One day Tschilper didn't make as much noise as usual and didn't want to leave his perch under the caravan. The next day, he didn't crow and didn't want to move.

In the late afternoon, Mutti tramped out to where Vati worked on the tractor. I sat on the ground behind the large tractor wheel, writing my newly learned words in the dirt with a stick.

"Tschilper is sick," Mutti said.

"Maybe it's just a chicken cold," Vati said.

"What can we do?"

"Why don't we wait a few days? He might just recover. And we can always eat him."

"We sure could use the meat," Mutti grumbled. "All I got from that order of chicks is expenses. And an unwanted pet. We didn't even get any eggs. But we can't just stand by and watch him suffer."

"I'll ask the local farmers. Maybe they know what to do."

"If we can't help him, we need to put him out of his misery. Whatever chicken sickness he has shouldn't affect the meat."

"Let's wait," Vati said.

Mutti nodded. "All right." Her footsteps receded.

I snuck away, afraid to let my parents know I overheard their conversation. I crawled under the caravan and wedged myself between the solid rubber tires. There, I folded my hands and asked God to make Tschilper feel better. I returned to the caravan with a lighter heart. Later that evening, in bed, I bent down from my top bunk and told Carmen, under me, that Mutti wanted us to eat Tschilper. Carmen's eyes grew wide, and her hand flew to her mouth.

"I don't believe you." She turned to the wall.

A few days later, Tschilper still hadn't recovered, despite my prayers. Mutti told Carmen to watch us and stay in the caravan. She hurried out toward Vati. We children crowded around the open caravan's door. We couldn't hear what they said, but things didn't bode well. Mutti stood with her feet apart and her hands on her hips, and Vati frowned and shook his head.

Mutti returned, pulled the large pot from under the gas stove, and poured water into it from the canister in the corner.

Carmen came into the kitchen from the living room. "What are you doing?"

Frowning at Carmen, Mutti placed the pot on a burner and said, "Shut up."

Outside, Vati strode toward the pack trailer and returned with an ax. He disappeared behind the caravan.

I glanced at Carmen. She bit her lip, her eyes wide and fearful. She glanced at Mutti, then back at me. I blinked because my eyes suddenly burned, and I felt like crying.

"Is Vati going to kill Tschilper?" Carmen whispered to me.

Mutti turned from the stove. "Tschilper isn't a pet," she said. "And besides, he's sick. He would just die by himself. This way he'll provide a good meal for us."

Carmen sobbed and ran into the living room. Josefa and I followed her. Together we huddled on the sofa and covered our ears so we wouldn't hear Tschilper cry.

I understood that we didn't always have much to eat, but in this case, I thought we should go hungry. We couldn't make a meal out of a friend, but Mutti insisted. In my eight-year-old mind, Mutti never made mistakes. Maybe I was stupid for thinking about Tschilper as a friend, but when I peered at Carmen, I knew she felt the same way.

Vati clumped up the caravan steps, holding a dead, headless rooster by its feet. I glanced at him and buried my face in my arms. This wasn't right, despite what Mutti said. I thought of Jesus, who loved everyone. Why hadn't he saved Tschilper?

Mutti poured the hot water over the dead rooster and plucked a fistful of brown feathers. We children rose as one and ran past her from the caravan. We hid behind the pack trailer. Maybe Mutti wouldn't find us and make us help.

When Mutti called us to come eat, we pretended not to hear. She found us behind the other caravan trailers, marched us home, and made us sit around the kitchen table. She placed a piece of fried chicken in front of each of us.

We stared at our plates, arms folded. Even little Franz, who always ate everything, refused to take a bite.

"Eat, you brats," Mutti said. "We don't have such good food all the time."

No one answered. I had no appetite, and I'm sure none of my siblings wanted to eat that day. We stared at the chicken and kept our mouths pressed shut.

Vati, who always ate so much, took a spoonful of mashed potatoes and pushed his plate away.

"I'm not hungry," he said and then got up from the table and went to tinker with some part of the merry-go-round.

Mutti pressed her lips together.

"You eat Tschilper, Mutti," Carmen ventured.

I expected Mutti to get mad, but she just stared at my sister.

"I have a stomachache," Mutti said in a small voice. She picked up her and Vati's untouched plates. "Go on out and play, then. Go, go," she said and shooed us from the caravan.

The remains of Tschilper disappeared without any of us having eaten a bite of him.

For a while, I struggled to understand why God hadn't saved Tschilper. Later I figured out the answer, but when I was eight, my faith wavered. I think how I must have felt the same way Mutti did most of her life.

Eventually I decided Tschilper was in heaven with God and Jesus, and he probably was happy there, even though, I was sure, he missed us.

That evening, when Mutti washed little Franz to get him ready for bed, we three girls sat crowded together on the converted bus seat, waiting our turn at the washbowl. None of us spoke. The kitchen was unnaturally quiet.

Mutti glanced at us, then back at Franz, whose face she wiped with a washrag. She said, "It's just as well we didn't eat Tschilper."

She paused. I bit my lip, Carmen fiddled with a strand of her hair, and Josefa sucked on her finger.

Mutti straightened and stared at us. "What's the matter with you all? Are you sick?"

Carmen shook her head.

"Well then," Mutti said. "Josefa, go wash." She sent Franz off, turned, and said, "Maybe we'll get another pet for you all. A real pet."

I sighed. A weight fell off my shoulders. Mutti accepted my feelings. But I didn't want another pet until, one day, we saw Vati talk to a local child that held something small, black and white, and very wiggly.

9

A MOVEABLE FEAST

MUTTI PICKS UP AN OLD BLACK-AND-WHITE PICTURE. OUR WHOLE family is depicted on it, even our little dog, the second pet we had.

"When your father first brought Wally home," Mutti says, "we were still so poor."

"But in spite of being so crowded and having no room for a pet, Wally was a great addition to the family," I say.

"That's what you kids thought," Mutti grumbles. "It was up to me to take care of her. Just one more responsibility added to everything I was already doing."

Thinking back now, I understand why Mutti wasn't all that happy when Wally joined our caravan. But for us kids, Wally became a wonderful friend.

SUMMER 1956

Carmen, Josefa, and I trudged home from school in some small village whose name I don't remember. We came to the marketplace, where our half-erected merry-go-round obscured a large oak next to our caravan. Vati was talking to a local boy who held something in his hands. He gave the boy free merry-go-round tickets in return for that something.

Vati turned to us and held up a small pup of indeterminate ancestry who couldn't keep still in his large hands. The little dog squirmed, trying

*This chapter received runner-up in the June 2006 Joyous Publishing Writing Contest

to lick his face. Her eyes were big and clear, and her tail wagged back and forth in a blur.

When she saw me, she stopped trying to lick Vati and seemed to smile. Mutti stepped from the open door of the caravan, wiped her hands on her apron, and took in the scene.

I thought of Tschilper. The memory still hurt, but this little doggie looked so nice. And it liked me. Perhaps God sent it to make me feel better. Maybe having a new pet wasn't such a bad idea.

But Mutti scowled. She must have forgotten she promised us another pet.

"What do you think you're doing?" she asked Vati. "I won't have a dog in the caravan. It's too small, and I don't need another mouth to feed. Take it back."

Vati held the dog tighter. "Be still, woman. Our son needs a dog, and he'll have a dog."

"Then you feed it and take care of it." Mutti turned her back on us.

Little Franz wandered down the steps and, with wide eyes, stared at the dog in Vati's hands. Vati bent and handed it to him. Four-year-old Franz hung on to the pup for a few seconds before she wiggled out of his grasp. Franz took a startled step back and grabbed a fistful of Mutti's skirt.

Vati shook his head and frowned at him. "You're a man, not a pansy. A real man isn't afraid of a little dog."

About to step into the caravan, Mutti turned to us. "He's just a little boy. Give him time. He'll get used to the dog."

The dog soon became everybody's friend. She never grew very big, but her curly black tail seldom quit wagging, and her perky little ears and short, black-and-white fur invited us to pet her. We called her Wally, after Caterina Valente, an Italian singer who had gorgeous brown eyes, just like our little dog.

That long ago, and so soon after World War II, we didn't have a lot of money and didn't always buy dog food. But Wally didn't care. She knew how to fend for herself. In every new town, when the fair started, Wally marched out of the caravan, down the four steps, and through the trampled grass between the attractions and the concessions. She slipped in and out between the crowd's legs, nose to the ground.

Her nose always led her to doggie treasures. At the corner of the brat-wurst stand, she'd discover a half-eaten bun, a bit of hot dog still in it, or a left-over dab of potato salad. Or she'd gnaw on a steak bone someone had thrown next to the trash can by the beer tent.

At the concession stands, Wally sat up on her hind legs, front paws neatly folded, and begged the fairgoers for pieces of *shashlik* [meat on a stick]. In a festive mood, the locals oohed and aahed over such a well-behaved little carnival dog and freely shared their bounty. And, if she wasn't full enough yet or was in the mood, Wally stooped to gobble a piece of candy or two, found near the cotton candy stand or the place that sold hot candied almonds.

More often than not, she didn't bother to eat the scraps from the table. She had so much better fare to choose from.

Wally was not dumb. She figured out soon that, if she buried her bones, they would be left behind when our caravan moved to the next town. And in the new town, she had a day or two before the feasting started again. So she decided to do something about that.

One day, when Vati broke down the merry-go-round, we heard him call Mutti.

"You have to come and see this," he said with a grin.

My sisters, Franz, and I trailed after Mutti. Vati took us to the pack trailer. The pack trailer had no windows, and at first we couldn't see anything, peering from sunny daylight into the dark trailer. Vati pointed to the pile of rags he kept in the corner to protect the merry-go-round pictures from getting scratched during transit. "I grabbed one of the rags to put between the pictures, and look at that."

Poking out from underneath the pile of rags were two bones and an assortment of half-eaten bratwurst. As if on cue, Wally hopped up into the trailer and dragged a bone outside to gnaw on. We decided to let her "bury" her treasures under the rags in the pack trailer from then on.

During the winters, life was harder for Wally. She gratefully ate our scraps, and Mutti begged for bones from the butcher to keep her going. But even in winter, Wally often found her own food. Once, when we had winter quarters close by a stream, Carmen came in on a cold December day and said, "You guys *have* to see what Wally is doing."

Josefa and I got up from our homework, slipped into our coats, and followed her to the stream behind our caravan. Crouched close to the water, Wally acknowledged us with a wag of her tail, but her eyes never left the water. Suddenly she swiped the water with a paw, and a fish flew out. Wally snapped at it and caught it between her jaws. Proudly she rose and carried the fish underneath our caravan, where she devoured it for supper.

Wally loved to chase. She didn't care whether it was a car or a chicken; she would see it and go after it. We always worried that she would get hit. When we caught her chasing cars, we'd whack her and yell at her, and she would droop her ears and pull her tail in. She seemed to understand. As soon as another car went by, though, Wally would prick up her ears, ready to go after it again. If one of us saw her, we warned her, "Wally, no."

She would hesitate, small body tensed, ready to go, and look around to see who warned her. If Vati or Mutti gave the warning, she slunk away and ignored the car. If one of us kids yelled at her, she pretended not to hear and bounded after it.

One day, Wally pricked up her ears at the sound of a car coming. She looked around. The only person in sight was my brother Franz. Franz yelled at her, and, as usual, Wally ignored him. The car roared down the road. As soon as it passed the spot where Wally stood, tense and anticipating, she bounded after it. Franz watched. He saw her getting too close. The car hit her, and she bounced off. Franz ran home with Wally drooped over his outstretched arms, her eyes rolled back into her head and her feet dangling lifelessly.

Mutti called Vati. Vati dropped his tools, ran to the pack trailer for an old blanket, bundled Wally into it, and drove her to the local vet. She was lucky and came home with only a broken leg. Eventually it healed. After that, when she ran fast, she limped on that leg.

Wally had learned her lesson. From then on, when she saw a car speed by, she pricked up her ears, then reconsidered and, in her noblest way, ignored this tempting thing running away from her, as if to let us know, "Car? What car? I didn't see a car!"

Chickens, though, were another thing. Many times, Vati placated an irate farmer and paid for a dead chicken. But once she had tasted chicken blood, Wally couldn't let the chickens be.

When we ran our attractions in a town's marketplace, no chickens or ducks would run around loose. But when our carnival entertained the locals in the commons, especially close to a pond, Wally would get into trouble.

One day Vati had enough. Wally had killed another chicken. She had gone a ways out, and we didn't know until the farmer showed up with the dead white bird hanging from its feet in his hand. Vati paid the farmer and asked for the chicken. After the farmer left, he approached Wally, holding the chicken by its feet.

"See this? Look at this," he said. Wally pulled in her tail. Vati reached out with the chicken and slapped Wally with it. The chicken's head connected with Wally's backside with a thump. Wally yipped and ran away, with Vati in hot pursuit. Vati's bowlegged gait made him look like a drunken sailor running after his ship. His white hair flew around his face, which was red from exertion. He slapped Wally again and again with the dead chicken. White feathers swirled around them. Every time the chicken's head connected with Wally, she let out a yelp. She finally found refuge under the caravan.

Wally deserved to be punished, but her yelps cut my heart. Maybe she had learned her lesson and Vati would leave her alone. But Vati crouched down, grabbed her by the nape of the neck and poked her face into the chicken.

"Don't you ever do that again," he said and then pulled her out from under the caravan and thrashed her again with the dead chicken.

By that time an audience of village children had formed. Careful to keep a respectful distance, they admired Vati's excellent work in dog training.

For the poor dog, it must have been a harsh lesson, but the lesson stuck. From then on Wally looked away whenever a chicken or duck meandered by, unaware of the potential danger to wing and life.

When Vati, sitting high on the tractor, pulled our caravan to the next town, I often sat in the corner by the kitchen window and watched the landscape roll by. Wally lay by my side or in my lap, shared my sandwich, and listened to my sorrows and wishes. She gave me a comforting lick just when I needed it, wagged her tail at all the right moments, smiled at me with her doggie smile, and licked my hand. Wally always understood. I still thank God for the blessing she was in the life of a lonely young girl.

10
SIBLINGS

MUTTI MARCHES INTO MY LARGE, BRIGHT KITCHEN AND, THROUGH the glass back door, observes the summer rain patter onto the grass and the daisies in the backyard. "Goodness, what a spacious place you have. You have it so much easier. How crowded we were in that caravan! I was always glad when I could get away from it all."

I didn't consider it cramped because it was the only way of life I knew. But I hated it when Mutti and Vati left.

Looking back, I realize Mutti didn't really have a choice but to leave us alone at home occasionally.

FEBRUARY 1957

I perched on the bus seat we used as a kitchen bench, finishing my homework. Mutti pushed past me and slipped into her fuzzy black coat hanging by the caravan door.

"You children behave," she said. "Vati and I will be back before supper."

She followed Vati out the door, and a blast of icy February wind rushed into the caravan. I shivered and

MUTTI AND KIDS

wished I lived in a real house, not a caravan; it was probably warmer in a house.

My last math problem was done, and I closed the book. For a moment I sat, not wanting to get up. I was nine years old, Carmen eleven. Josefa was just a year younger than me, and Franz was almost seven. Except for Eva, only three, we were big enough to take care of ourselves, but I still hated it when Vati and Mutti left. They were going to scout out one of the towns where we would hold our traveling carnival the next summer. I wondered why Vati couldn't go by himself and let Mutti stay home with us.

I slid from the bench and took my favorite doll, the one with curly red hair and a blue dress, from the toy drawer next to the food cupboard. Josefa came through the open sliding doors from the living room.

"I wanted to play with that doll." She grabbed at it. "Give it to me, dummy."

"I'm not a dummy!" I yelled and held the doll up, out of her reach.

Franz followed Josefa. He laughed. "You're a loudmouth."

Eva came up behind Franz. He pushed her. She tumbled onto her bottom and started crying.

"Stop it, everybody!" I screamed louder than before.

"Shut up, loudmouth," Carmen yelled.

Why did they keep teasing me, when I told them in my loudest voice to stop? I wanted to be friends with my sisters and brother, but they always called me names. I opened my mouth to let my sister know she was a dummy too and I hated her.

Something made me stop, though.

I furrowed my brow and dropped my hand. Josefa pried the doll from my fingers, and I let her. Eva stopped crying, got up, and went to inspect the open toy drawer. Franz looked at me, eyes wide and mouth open, and then returned to the wooden blocks dotting the linoleum floor in the living room.

Yelling never did any good. Maybe I could try something different. I could go off by myself and read. It would be better than being teased. Reading, I'd be alone, but I felt alone anyway. I couldn't think of another way to stop them fighting with me.

In the living room, Josefa yelled at Carmen, and I realized they wouldn't be kind today. It would be better to be alone. Then I remembered Jesus. I could always talk to him when I felt lonely. I reached under the kitchen table for my satchel and pulled out the reader.

With my lips pressed together to keep in the names *Dummkopf* [stupid head] and *Blödmann* [dummy], which I wanted to call my siblings, I marched past them into the bedroom at the other end of our home and slammed the door shut. In the bedroom, I plopped onto the bottom bunk and opened the book.

On my bunk, the book on my lap, I read the same words over and over. My thoughts kept returning to my sisters and brother. I told myself yelling wouldn't make them love me. I bowed my head, folded my hands, and said a prayer for Jesus to help me feel happy. Then I tried again to read my story.

Soon I started to shiver. Goose bumps formed on my thin arms, and my feet turned icy. I hugged myself, but then I couldn't read. I took my book, cracked the door open enough to squeeze through, and pushed by Franz and Eva on my way to the warm kitchen, where I sat in the corner of the kitchen bench, my book before me.

Josefa trailed me, calling, *"Klappe! Klappe!* [Loudmouth! Loudmouth!]"

I pretended I didn't hear her and focused on the words in the book. After a short time, she stopped, and I got involved with my story. When I looked up after maybe half an hour, the others sat on the floor and the sofa in the living room, squabbling, and seemed to have forgotten about me.

It wasn't cold in the kitchen, but I sat in my corner, hugging myself. The book wasn't interesting anymore. I wanted to get up and see what my sisters and brother were doing. Maybe they'd be glad to see me.

I rose, but then I sat down again and told myself to remember their teasing. So I wouldn't feel so alone, I closed my eyes and thought of Jesus, his friendly face smiling at me.

Josefa's shriek from the living room interrupted my reading. Carmen yelled at her, and Franz laughed. I listened to the commotion, safely tucked into my corner. Wally hopped onto the bench next to me. I made room for her. She probably didn't like the fighting, either. I petted her, picked up the book, and found my place in the story.

After a few minutes, Carmen wandered in.

"What are you doing?" she asked.

"Reading."

Carmen pulled her book from her satchel. "I'm going to read too."

"Me too," Josefa announced and sat on the other side of the table.

"Me too," Eva said. She took my math book that still lay on the table and looked at the pages.

Together we sat around the kitchen table, peacefully reading. Franz drove a toy car through his blocks, making car sounds that accompanied our small reading group.

Before we knew it, the caravan swayed to the sound of feet coming up the steps. Vati and Mutti were back. My sisters looked up and smiled at me. I grinned back and put away my book.

But not all our times alone together had such good endings. About a year later, things turned out a lot scarier. That afternoon, Mutti put on her coat with the black fur collar and took her purse from the kitchen counter. Vati was already outside, starting the old VW. Mutti told us to be good and not get into trouble, and that they'd be back in the evening. Then they left.

I decided to draw a large daisy that I had seen last summer in someone's front yard. I leaned over the kitchen table and dug in my satchel for paper and some colored pencils.

Next to me, Josefa pushed a wooden blue car across the table. She bumped it into my satchel. I moved the satchel to the side.

"Leave me alone," I said, but she turned the car and did it again. I squeezed into the corner, picked up my satchel, and held it up.

Franz took my spot. He grabbed at Josefa's toy car. Josefa screamed and hit him with both fists. Carmen, trying to settle things, also hit Franz. Franz returned the blow, and Carmen stepped into the living room.

I stood in the corner, held my satchel high, and bit my lip. I wished I were outside, but in order to leave, I needed to push through my screaming and hitting siblings and would probably get caught in their fight. Rather than risk that, I stayed squeezed in my corner.

Eva stepped through the half-open sliding-glass door that separated the kitchen from the living room. Carmen bumped into her, and in the cramped surroundings, Eva slipped and fell against the glass door. She flailed backward. Her bare heel kicked the glass hard. The sound of glass shattering, almost melodic, stilled all other noise.

A heartbeat later, a spray of crimson colored the glass shards. Blood dripped from a gash in little Eva's foot. Eva's scream ripped through the momentary quiet.

Blood and broken glass sprinkled the linoleum and the toys on the floor. I dropped my satchel. It thumped onto the bloody glass. My hands grew cold, and I started shaking. Panic squeezed my chest. What if my little sister died? Maybe I was to blame for this accident. Mutti always reminded me of how clumsy I was.

I took a step closer to Eva and reached out my shaking hand. When I saw her panicked face, I didn't know what to do. Mutti and Vati were gone, and nobody was here to fix things. My heart raced, as if it was trying to burst out of my body, and I couldn't breathe. When I finally caught my breath, I joined Eva in her screams. Josefa wailed.

Carmen yelled over the noise for us to shut up. I stared at her and clamped my mouth shut. Carmen was here. She would know what to do.

She shooed all of us except Eva into the back of the living room, where the glass hadn't fallen. With Eva's sobs accompanying her frantic actions, she dug in the first aid drawer in the kitchen. She found a large, sticky bandage and plastered it on Eva's heel. The bleeding stopped.

Carmen and Eva joined us in the living room, where I cowered with the equally subdued Josefa and Franz. Carmen turned on the radio. Together we sat in a tight clump, listening to a German translation of "The Shadow." For once, we were nice to each other until Vati and Mutti came home.

After we told her what happened, Mutti peeled back the bandage on Eva's foot, decided the cut wasn't so bad and would heal just fine, and sent us all to bed.

Half asleep, I remembered another accident. At least Eva didn't have to go to the hospital, as I had to that time.

11

AN ACCIDENT

I LOOK FOR MY GLASSES AND FINALLY FIND THEM IN THE BATHROOM. I put them on and join Mutti at the front door. She is ready to go out and see some more of Utah.

"You still don't wear glasses," I say as we leave the house. "You have excellent eyesight."

"It wasn't that great a few years ago," she says. "But since the glaucoma operation, I can see much better." She takes in my glasses. "You would have great eyesight too if it weren't for the accident. You were always an accident-prone child."

Thinking back, I guess I had no more accidents than other children. But that incident with my eyes had been traumatic.

SUMMER 1956

I was nine that summer. I found ten pfennig and, at one of the stands that sold sweets and toys, bought a small, blue plastic bow and arrow. The arrow had a bit of rubber on its tip and actually stuck to things if you shot it just right. I wandered around outdoors, looking for places to shoot my arrow, when Franz came up to me. He reached for my toy. "What do you have there?"

I pulled my hand away. "A bow and arrow. It really works."

"That's a toy for boys. You're just a girl. Give it to me."

I hid it behind my back. "It's mine."

My brother grabbed my hand from behind. "I want it!"

"No!" I screamed and pulled away.

Franz was a big six-year-old to my skinny nine-year-old frame. He grabbed me around the waist, pried my fingers open, and took my little bow away from me. The arrow fell from my hand.

Franz held up the bow. "I got it now. It's mine!"

"Give it back! Give it back!" I screamed. I turned my fingers into claws, trying to scratch him so he'd give me back my toy, but he held it up. I reached for it. My fingers brushed the cool plastic, but Franz pulled away and broke it in two.

A sudden, sharp pain ripped through my right eye. It felt as if someone poked it with a hot needle. I let go of Franz.

"There's something in my eye!" I screamed. "It hurts really bad!"

The pain rushed in waves from my eye through my head and my whole body. I squeezed my eye shut, but the pain didn't diminish. I stumbled home, the toy forgotten.

Mutti stirred a pot of soup on the gas stove.

Tears streamed from my eye. It felt as if a knife was stuck in it. I clapped my hand over the hot, tender eye and screamed, "My eye, my eye! It hurts."

Mutti dropped the wooden spoon into the soup. "Let me look at it." She pulled my hand away. "I can't see anything. Just give it some time. If you quit carrying on so, it will quit hurting. What happened, anyway?"

"I was playing with my new bow and arrow, and Franz took it away from me and broke it," I said between sobs. "I think a piece flew into my eye."

Mutti returned to the oxtail soup, my favorite, but I hardly noticed. The pain in my eye didn't lessen.

"It must have come out again," Mutti said. "I can't see anything in your eye."

I sat on the chair, hugging myself and trying not to cry too loudly. By the time Mutti placed lunch on the table, it still hurt the same. I whimpered.

Vati asked why I was crying, and Mutti told him I had gotten something in my eye.

I couldn't eat. My whole face hurt, and every time I moved, a stab of pain pierced my eye.

Vati finished eating and rose, turning to me. "Let me take a look."

I gasped for breath between sobs and pulled my hand from the eye.

"Open it," he ordered. I did, and it hurt all over again. He peered into

it, turning my head this way and that way. "I can't see anything, either."
He let go of my head.

Tears streamed down my cheeks.

"Don't carry on so," Vati said. "It can't be that bad. Just go to bed.
When you wake again, it will be okay."

It hurt badly. But Vati and Mutti probably were right. They always
told me I was overly sensitive. In the morning I would surely feel better.

For once I didn't complain. I pulled my nightgown from the dresser
drawer in the bedroom, undressed quickly, slipped into it, and crawled
under the feather cover. I couldn't sleep, so I prayed to God to help the
pain go away. But it didn't. Pain throbbed in my eye and only lessened if
I didn't move my eye under my eyelids. Between tears and moans I dozed
off and on, wondering why God didn't help. Maybe I should have let
Franz keep the toy. I promised to be nicer next time and turned to find a
more comfortable position.

Every once in a while, one of my siblings would tell me to be quiet,
but one by one they all went to sleep and left me in my half-awake misery.

Finally, light dawned. It didn't occur to me to leave my bed until my
parents started making noises in the living room. Then I got up, pulled
yesterday's dress over my head, and entered the living room, hand clasped
over my swollen eye.

Mutti took one look at me. "Goodness, you're still crying! Does it
still hurt?"

I nodded, and she turned to Vati. "We need to take this child to a
doctor."

Vati looked me over without touching my hot face. "Let's go," he said.

12

AWAY FROM HOME

MUTTI AND I ARE AT THE DEPARTMENT STORE, LOOKING FOR A birthday present for my husband's granddaughter. We wander among the aisles, which are crowded with dolls in all sizes and colors. I pick a large, blonde one from the shelf, dressed in a fluffy blue skirt.

"Hmm. This one is too fancy for a two-year-old." I put it back.

"I remember the first time I ever bought a brand-new doll for one of my children," Mutti says. "I bought it for you. We had no money for such extras, but at the time it seemed more important than food."

"I remember too," I said. "I was so happy to see you. And the doll was so beautiful."

"I felt sorry for you, and I wanted to lighten up your stay in the hospital. Your father said we needed the money for more important things, like feeding you all, but I insisted."

I smile at Mutti. She must have cared deeply. She usually gave in to Vati, in spite of his quiet ways, but that time she didn't.

SUMMER 1956

I stood in the kitchen, hand clasped to my hot face, while Mutti combed through her hair and put some lipstick on.

"Carmen, take care of the kids." She grabbed my hand, and we bumbled down the steps.

Vati, already outside, had asked a man where the local doctor's office was. When we came out, he turned and strode along the sidewalk, swaying from side to side in his sailor's gait. Mutti and I hurried after him.

In the medical office not too far away, the doctor took a look at my swollen face, gently pried my hand away, and inspected my eye. He rose and turned to my parents. "The cornea is injured. The best I can do is cover it up. You need to go to the hospital. It needs an operation."

An operation? I wondered what that was. It sounded scary and painful. In addition to the pain in my eye, my empty stomach clenched up.

The doctor gave Vati the address to the hospital in Giessen. "They have a very good optical department at the university hospital. They'll fix her up again."

Vati frowned. "If that's what has to be, I'd better take her there."

We walked back to the caravan, and Vati hurried us into the car. "I don't have all day," he muttered. "I still have to put up the merry-go-round."

I was sorry to keep Vati away from the merry-go-round, but mostly I was tightly wrapped in my own misery.

I didn't see much of the hospital since my bad eye was covered and I had to hurry to keep up with Mutti and Vati. But it smelled funny there, like medicine. Humming noises and the sounds of many people calling and talking surrounded me. People hurried to and fro, some of them in wheelchairs. It seemed like a big city, except that it was inside. I remembered getting lost with Josefa the winter before. My heartbeat sped up, and I hurried to catch up with Mutti. I didn't want to be lost there.

Mutti stopped and opened a door to a small room containing a large desk. A wrinkle-faced man in a white coat gave me a pill to swallow with a small cup of water. I didn't want to swallow the pill. Beside the pain in my hurt eye, my good eye stung with suppressed tears. I stared at the doctor.

Behind his glasses, the doctor's kind eyes smiled at me. "This will make you feel better. Go ahead. It tastes like candy."

I swallowed the pill. He was right; it tasted sweet.

The doctor asked me to sit on a bed. He gently pulled the bandage off my bad eye and shined a light into it.

It hurt even more, and I drew back. The doctor let go of my face. Mutti always said I cried too much. So I swallowed my tears. My eye seemed to hurt a little less all of a sudden.

"Tsk, tsk," the doctor said. "We need to operate."

I had a vague idea that an operation would include cutting into a person. I balled my fist. In spite of my efforts to hold it back, a tear leaked from my good eye.

The doctor turned to a woman in a nurse's uniform. "Take her to the children's ward. We'll operate first thing in the morning."

The nurse took my hand. I turned to Mutti. I wanted to go home, not be operated on. "It doesn't hurt so much now," I said. "Can I go home with you?"

"You have to stay," Mutti said. "The doctor has to fix your eye, and then we'll come and get you."

I wanted to cry again, but I had no tears left. I swallowed, then yawned. My body was heavy, and I dragged my feet.

Mutti patted my hand. "Go with that nice nurse. She'll take care of you. We'll be back as soon as we can."

The nurse told me to call her Nurse Sigrid. I allowed her to lead me off. One last time, I turned to look at my mother and father. Vati had his back to me and was talking to the doctor, but just then, Mutti turned and gave me one last reassuring smile.

Nurse Sigrid, a young woman with warm, blue eyes, took me to a room and helped me get into bed. She smiled and told me I would be all right. The pain was a distant, suppressed thrumming waiting to flare up again. But for the moment, it was under control. Under the blankets in my bed, I folded my hands and whispered, "Jesus don't let the pain come back. Bless Mutti and Vati, and don't let them forget me. Amen."

Before I could worry what would happen to me, I was asleep.

The next morning, I ate a fresh bun with butter for breakfast. Nurse Sigrid gave me some medicine and made me lie on a bed with wheels. I didn't want to, but she told me it would be fun to be wheeled while lying in a bed. So I did it, and the nurse was right.

She wheeled me along the hallway. I wished Vati and Mutti could see me being rolled on a bed, but I told myself they couldn't because they needed to work. Vati needed to put up the merry-go-round, and Mutti needed to tend my sisters and brother. Nevertheless, I pushed myself up on my elbows and looked around, just in case.

Some of the doors along the hallway stood open, others were closed. People in nightgowns walked past my bed on wheels, and I recognized some people as nurses because of their uniforms. But I didn't see anybody I knew. My good eye stung, and I swallowed a sob. I grabbed for the nurse's hand. When I thought about the doctor operating on my eye, my heart pounded.

I asked Nurse Sigrid where we were going.

"To the operating room. It won't hurt at all; you'll see. You can even see what the doctors are doing because there is a mirror on the ceiling. But you don't have to look if you don't want to."

"Are you sure it won't hurt?"

Nurse Sigrid pressed my hand and smiled. "I'm sure. It might feel a bit cold, but it won't hurt."

Nurse Sigrid rolled me into another room, where she put me on a different bed. Something soft pushed against my forehead. I couldn't move my head when I tried. My nurse stood beside me, her warm hand around my cold fingers. I hung on to her hand, and she gave it a reassuring squeeze. "Don't worry. The doctor needs your head to be very still, so he's holding it with these clamps. Are they too tight?"

I tried to shake my head but couldn't, so I said, "No."

Nurse Sigrid held my hand, and I watched the bald head of the doctor in the round mirror on the ceiling. The mirror looked strange, like a funhouse mirror, and I didn't see a lot since I couldn't move my head, just the doctor's hands out of the corner of my good eye. But the nurse was right; it didn't hurt at all. Something cold touched my cheek around the eye. I felt nothing else.

The doctor finished, put a bandage on my right eye, loosened the clamps from my head, and patted my cheek. "You've been very brave. It won't hurt anymore now. In a few days, we'll take off the bandage."

My bad eye was covered, but I saw fine out of the other one. The wheels on the bed squeaked when the nurse pushed me back to my room. The white walls moved past me. She put me to bed and sat by me until I fell asleep.

The next day was Sunday. The families of the other two children in my room came. People moved in and out of the room, bringing candy and toys. A little sister and brother played around the room talking and sometimes yelling. I watched them, alone in my bed in the corner.

I told myself Mutti and Vati were working and would come on Tuesday or Wednesday, when things weren't so busy. But it didn't help. My heart ached. I thought of Jesus and that he loved me. He would make sure Mutti would come for me soon.

To distract myself, I played with my fingers. I wanted to see them double, like I had so many times in the past. This time they stayed single, however, no matter how I tried to see them. I looked up. Nurse Sigrid made her way past the other child's mother and around a little boy toward my bed. "You poor thing," she said when she arrived in my corner. She patted my head and gave me a small hard lemon candy. I sucked the candy and smiled at her.

Early the next day, I heard footsteps, and Vati and Mutti walked into the room, waking me up.

Mutti searched the room, spied me in the corner bed, and came toward me. Vati followed after her and sat in a bedside chair.

"Oh, Sonjalein," Mutti said, using the endearment form of Sonja. "They have bandaged your eye. Does it still hurt?"

I smiled and shook my head. "Can I go home now?"

"Not yet," Vati said. "The doctor said you need to stay a while longer. They still have to take the stitches out of your eye."

I nodded. I didn't quite understand what Vati was talking about, but I wasn't scared anymore. Taking out stitches would probably be just like the operation. And that hadn't hurt at all.

"I brought you something." Mutti handed me a box wrapped in brown paper.

I took the box and unwrapped it, every few seconds glancing up to make sure Mutti was still there.

I opened the box and forgot to breathe. The prettiest doll I had ever seen smiled her painted dolly smile at me, and she looked brand new. She wore a crisply starched white-and-blue gingham dress with a small, red flower embroidered under the white collar.

The doll was all pink and rosy, with her blonde hair and blue eyes under thick, black eyelashes. I took her from the box and held her close. Such a special present, like a gift for a princess. Sunshine, warmth, and safety surrounded me. Mutti smiled at me, and I smiled back. I must have been a good girl sometime because Mutti brought me this beautiful doll. What a wonderful feeling it was to know Mutti loved me, almost better than when I thought of Jesus loving me.

I hugged the doll, my eyes never leaving Mutti. She must have missed me too. I hoped I could go home with her now. The hospital was okay, and the nurse was nice, but I wanted to be home.

Mutti showed me how the doll closed its eyes when laid on its back. It even said, "Mama."

"What are you going to name her?" Mutti asked.

I thought about it. "Maybe Sigrid. She looks just like Nurse Sigrid. She takes care of me."

Mutti asked me about the hospital, the nurses, and my eye. Vati went outside to use the bathroom.

When Vati returned, Mutti told me to be good and that they would come back in a few days to take me home. She smiled at me. She was much prettier than my nurse.

They left the room. The door sighed shut. I watched it for a while. Maybe they would return and take me home after all. But the door stayed closed. I turned to my new doll and pushed a curl from her forehead. Soon I was busy with Sigrid, moving her arms and legs and turning her over and over so she'd say, "Mama."

A few days later, when my bandage came off, I thought for a moment I could see normally, until I closed my left eye and tried to see with only my right eye. Everything disappeared. Fuzziness filled the room, as if I were looking with my good eye through the bottom of a soda bottle. All I saw were colors and large shapes. For a moment, my heart beat faster and my chest felt tight, but when I opened my other eye, everything went back to normal. I was already used to things looking a bit flatter and not as sharp as before the accident, but that was okay. I could still see.

After Vati and Mutti took me home, I wore a black patch over my right eye for what seemed an eternity. Every morning and night, I put drops into my eye. They felt cold and uncomfortable and kept running down my cheeks.

* * *

Over the years, my right eye wandered more and more because I never used it to focus. When I was fifteen, Mutti told me this eye, always on its own, was too ugly. She took me to an eye doctor, who decided a small operation, done in his office, would take care of it.

Besides shortening the muscles that moved the eye, he must have taken scar tissue off the pupil because after the operation I saw much better.

The optometrist in Wetzlar sent Mutti and me to Giessen to get an invention from America that would help me focus and see better.

"It's called a contact lens," he said to Mutti. "It's a small glass disc made to be put directly onto the eye. It will help your daughter to see almost normally again with this eye."

This we did. The optometrist in Giessen was proud to be the first German to have contact lenses available to people who might need them. "And you surely need one," he told me. He taught me how to insert the lens with a small rubber pipette.

I went home and faithfully wore the contact lens. With the lens, every time I got something, even a speck of dust, in my eye, it hurt badly. I soon learned to take out the lens and suck it clean before reinserting it.

I wore the lens for a few years, but the sight in my bad eye didn't improve much. My appearance did, however. Even now, people hardly can tell I have a non-functioning eye. Only when I get tired does my eye wander a little, just as my accent does.

13

DAILY LIFE

THE LAST NOTES OF *LA BOHÈME* WIND TO THEIR END AT THE OPEN-air concert. People rise from their seats or from the blankets on the grass and applaud. When the young performers leave, we get up from our wooden bench and wander toward the parking lot in the waning evening light.

Mutti surveys the crowd. "I went to the opera a lot before I met your father. My mother inherited some money from my father, you know. We lived in an expensive apartment and even had a telephone. That was rare in those days. I wish I would have had that space and comfort when you children were small." She sighs. "When the weather was bad, all you children squeezed into the caravan. I hardly had room to sit. And the noise! If you could have been a bit more spread out, the noise wouldn't have been so bad."

I agree with her. A phone in our caravan would have been unthinkable. We did have electricity, but only when Vati connected it after we arrived in the next town.

We also went shopping daily because we simply had no room to store food.

SUMMER 1956

Evening darkness descended upon a drizzly Tuesday. We'd arrived in Oberbiel, a small town in the center of Germany, late that afternoon. Vati placed our caravans on the edge of the town square in the middle of the village. He would erect our attractions the next day in the center of the square.

Vati already had the power connected, and the light on the ceiling dispelled the darkness in our caravan. Two US Army canisters Vati had bought from some *Besetzungssoldaten* [US Army soldiers] years ago served as our water supply. Now Vati took the empty canisters and filled them at the well in the center of the town square.

Since we didn't own a refrigerator, Mutti sent Carmen to the butcher on the corner of the town square to buy two Marks' worth of sandwich meats for supper. She handed me the milk can, a few coins, and four merry-go-round tickets.

"Go to the farmer across the street," she said, "and get a pail of milk. If he's interested, pay with the tickets. Or give him the money."

One of us bought milk almost every night, and Mutti was always happy if we got the milk without paying for it. I took the pail, the tickets, and the money. I didn't want to go to a new place and meet more strangers, but I tried to persuade myself that perhaps this time I would get to see what the inside of a house looked like.

Mutti pushed me out of the door. "Go on already."

German farmhouses were built in town rather than in the countryside. The farmhouse was usually in a large yard close to the barn where the livestock was housed every night. During evenings in the summer, we often heard the sound of cowbells and the mooing from the cows coming home to the barn from their grazing.

I wandered across the cobblestone street into the spacious farmyard. What would the farmer be like? Would he be impatient or not give me any milk? I wished Mutti had asked Josefa to go.

The farmer's house was on one side of the yard, and the barn on the other. Chickens wandered across my way, clucking and pecking at the ground. A large, orange cat slunk through the half-open barn door.

I stood in front of the house door for a long moment and finally knocked. The farmer's wife, in a dress and a blue apron, answered. When she saw me, she smiled. "Hi! Can I help you?" Her smile never left her face.

A weight fell from my shoulders. I peeked around her heavy frame and spied a cross with Jesus hanging from it on the hallway wall. Again I wondered what it would be like to live in a house and not have to travel all the time. I would have friends for a long time, not just for a few days. And maybe, if I had a farmer's wife for a mother, she'd be happy when

I prayed. After all, she had a cross with Jesus on her wall. We only had Vati's violins on ours.

I smiled back at the farmer's wife. "I'm from the carnival. I'd like to buy a pail of milk, if you please."

"Go over to the barn. My husband is just finishing the milking. He'll sell you some."

I went into the warm, dark barn and wrinkled my nose. It smelled like warm milk, hay, and cows, all mixed together. Cows and horses rustled in their pens. A clean, wide aisle separated the pens, and the concrete floor was freshly washed. In one of the pens, the farmer straddled a stool beside a cow. His fingers curled around two teats, alternating, one hand up and the other down, stroking the teats with smooth, sure motions.

I told him what I wanted, and he said to wait a moment. The foamy milk streamed from the cow's udder into the bucket in a steady rhythm. When the foam of the milk lapped the rim of the bucket, the farmer patted the cow, got up, and poured the milk through a sieve into a shiny metal container like my pail, but much larger.

He ladled some of the creamy white liquid into my pail and took my tickets. "The grandchildren will be happy," he said and waved me off with one hand. I left, thinking about what he said. I had a grandmother in Poland and one in Berlin, but I'd never seen them. I was sure a farmer like him would make a nice grandfather.

I trekked home, holding the milk can carefully so it wouldn't spill.

I arrived home, and Mutti grabbed the pail from me and poured the milk into cups, one for each child. I sat on the bus seat, eating my sandwich and staring out the window. The stars were coming out, and a few dim streetlights turned on. How still and peaceful it looked!

After supper, Mutti diapered Eva and slipped her nightgown over the diaper. "Children, go to bed," she told us.

First Franz and Josefa washed their hands and faces in the kitchen, in the same bowl Mutti used during the day to wash dishes. When it was my turn, I shivered, and goose bumps rose on my bare arms. I touched the cold, wet washcloth and rubbed it across my face. Then I dipped the tips of my cold fingers into the icy water and decided not to brush my teeth. Mutti didn't always notice if we didn't brush them every day, anyway.

I poured the water into the refuse bucket behind the little curtain by the outside door. In the bucket, potato peels and other organic stuff collected until it filled up or until one of us went to the bathroom in it. Then we dumped the bucket out into any weeds we could find.

A thin, Indian-patterned rug covered the linoleum on the living room floor. Mutti occasionally took it outside, hung it over a fence, and beat it with a carpet beater. We didn't own a vacuum, but eventually Mutti bought a sweeper for the carpet.

I trudged through the living room, dragging my feet over the rug and wishing I could stay up longer. When I pulled the bedroom door open and breathed in the smell, I wrinkled my nose.

The galvanized diaper bucket, filled with bleach water, stood in a corner of our bedroom, and the smell of baby urine and bleach wafted through its closed lid. Every night when I went to bed, the smell struck me, but after a few minutes I didn't notice it anymore.

I wondered if the farmer's house smelled of diapers too.

14

DRIVING LESSONS

W'RE IN OREGON, GETTING READY TO TAKE A TRIP TO THE beach at Seaside. Mutti climbs into the front of the van, next to Ken. I get in the back and remind Mutti to use her seat belt. She fumbles with it until it clicks in.

"We didn't have seat belts when I was younger," she mutters. "And nobody ever died."

Ken starts the motor and eases into traffic.

"I remember when you first drove our car," I say to Mutti. "You didn't even have a driver's license then."

"I got that later," Mutti says. "But I haven't used it for a long time."

"You don't need to in Germany. It's so much easier and less trouble to use public transportation. Why did you decide to get your driver's license in the first place?"

"That was all your father's fault," Mutti says. "He could make me so mad. It wasn't easy to keep things going in our caravan. I had such a hard time getting him to help when I needed it."

Ken turns onto the highway, and I think back. I was there the first time Mutti drove a car.

SUMMER 1956

One sunny morning, Mutti lugged the diaper pail from our bedroom outside into the sunshine. I followed her to escape the noise and commotion.

She poured the stinking liquid into the weeds behind the caravan. Mutti put the pail with the wet diapers next to the stairs, went back in, and dragged the pot with boiling water from the gas stove out to the bucket. She poured some detergent and the scalding hot water over the diapers and stirred them around with an old wooden spoon until the water cooled. Then she washed and rinsed them, and wrung them out by hand.

I lost interest watching her. A stick in the grass caught my attention, and I threw it for Wally to chase.

"Sonja," Mutti called. "Come here and hang up these diapers." She pointed to a nearby fence.

I threw the stick one last time and ran to get the bucket.

Mutti stretched. "It's time for the rest of the laundry," she muttered. Shouts and yells exploded through the open caravan door.

"Dang brats," Mutti said and hurried toward the never-ending commotion.

I hung the diapers and returned to the caravan with the empty bucket. Carmen swiped the wet gray dishrag back and forth over the kitchen table. Breadcrumbs rained onto the floor.

Most of the time, we kept the door from the bedroom to the living room closed, but today it stood wide open. Mutti knelt on the floor in the bedroom, digging in the dirty clothes drawer under the triple bunk beds.

"Josefa, take Eva and Franz outside," she shouted over her shoulder. "The sun is shining."

Josefa picked up little Eva and squeezed by me. Franz ran ahead outside.

I set the pail by the bedroom door so it wouldn't be in Mutti's way. Mutti pulled out a used duvet, a cover for a feather quilt, and stuffed everybody's dirty clothes into it. My favorite dress disappeared into the duvet.

Mutti dragged the duvet through the living room and kitchen and down the stairs. I followed her. She dropped the duvet to the ground next to our VW. She turned, looked around, and marched to the half-erected merry-go-round. Eva sat in the grass by the merry-go-round, picking the small white and yellow weeds we called goose flowers. Close to her, Josefa tussled with Wally. I couldn't see Franz. Mutti walked past the pack trailer toward the tractor, and there was Vati with Franz, who was standing at attention and poking his finger through the hole in a wrench.

"Pilzchen," Mutti said. "I need to take the laundry to the wash woman."

"Not now. I'm busy." Vati's head disappeared under the hood of the tractor.

"I can't get all this stuff there by myself," Mutti pointed to the duvet full of dirty clothes. "I need you to drive me."

"Not now. I'll do it tomorrow."

Mutti stood straighter and put her hands on her hips. "You always say that. If you had your way, we'd never wear clean clothes. If you won't take me, I'll have to do it myself."

"Go ahead," Vati said, frowning. "Have it your way. The keys are in the car."

Mutti's lips tightened, and her black eyes iced up. She marched back to the VW and opened the door. She dragged the laundry into the backseat, slipped behind the steering wheel, and slammed the door shut.

Through the open car window, I saw her fumble with the key. Finally the old car sputtered into life, jumped, and died.

Mutti's hands grasped the steering wheel as if it were a lifesaver. She gave Vati a beseeching look.

Vati grinned and returned to the tractor.

Mutti frowned and said something I didn't catch. She loosened her hands from the steering wheel and turned the key again. This time, the car jumped to life and kept purring. Her lips pressed together, Mutti turned the steering wheel. The VW jumped and died again.

Mutti sat still. She stared at Josefa and me. Her brow furrowed under her dark curls.

I wondered what she was thinking. Mutti used to steer the car when we traveled. She never had any problems then. But when Vati moved the carnival, the car was connected to the caravan with a stiff metal bar and didn't need to be turned on. It surely would be more difficult to drive with the car running.

Mutti bent her head and once more fumbled with the key. The car sputtered. She switched it off. A moment later, she tried again. This time the engine caught and settled into a smooth purr.

Mutti sat behind the steering wheel, one hand on each side. Once again, she glanced over at where Vati's behind stuck out from under the tractor's hood. Vati didn't look back. Mutti slammed the door shut and turned the steering wheel, very slowly this time. Nothing happened. Suddenly the VW sputtered, jumped, and inched away from the caravan. Her face screwed up in concentration, hands clamped on each side of the steering wheel, Mutti eased the car onto the street.

Vati's head came out from under the tractor. He stood straight and turned. Mutti had maneuvered the VW around a corner and disappeared from sight. He grinned, shook his head, and patted a cigarette from the pack he took out of his breast pocket.

Mutti returned half an hour later, the laundry safely delivered, and the car still in one piece.

From then on, Mutti drove the laundry herself. Eventually a policeman stopped her and asked why she was going so slowly. When she explained she had no driver's license, he admonished her to get one soon, so that winter Mutti took lessons and got her license.

* * *

Now, strapped into the seat belt in my van, I smile to myself. Things were a lot simpler when I was small. I don't think if she were to drive without a license today she'd get away with just a stern warning.

15

SCHOOL

MUTTI STEPS DOWN THE STAIRS, MOVING LIKE THE MODEL SHE once was. She's dressed in her black-and-red bathing suit, ready to go to the pool with me. She puts her towel on the glass coffee table. "I just remembered. It's your sister's birthday today. Carmen is turning fifty-nine. Why don't we call her before we go?"

"It's a little too late," I answer. "It's probably past midnight in Germany right now. Let's write her an email instead." I place my bag next to Mutti's towel and head to the computer in the living room. Mutti follows.

"How do you know how late it is in Germany?"

"It's easy. Just add eight hours to the time it is here, and that's the time it would be in Germany."

I sit down and pull a chair next to me for Mutti.

"You're all so smart." She sits beside me. "Carmen, Eva, and Franz have their own businesses. Josefa is married to a rich engineer. With the kind of education you children received, I'd never have thought you all would become so successful."

"It wasn't that bad," I say. "I even sometimes made friends."

Mutti shakes her head. "Vati and I always taught you not to associate with those dumb, inbred cow-town kids. You never listened."

I mentally shrug. Mutti and I have argued about that before. It won't do any good. She convinced herself a long time ago that anyone from a small town is mentally defective. I suppose that is because she was born and raised in the greatest European city of her time, Berlin. But even as a child, I didn't quite believe that people who lived in small towns were inferior.

I start the computer and think back to when I was small and went to school during the summers. Unlike here in the United States, the German kids got two small vacations, one in the spring and one in the fall. We carnival kids went to school in a different town every week or two in the summers.

SUMMER 1957

One Wednesday morning, we arrived in another town. That afternoon Mutti called Carmen and me. "You'll all go to school tomorrow. Go, find some local children and ask when and where school is held."

Carmen ran the toe of her shoe through the dirt on the linoleum floor. It made a scraping noise. "Do we have to go? Those dumb local kids always stare at us."

I thought about last week's school. By the time I finally got used to their way of doing things, the teacher had the kids practice the songs they had to sing for the fair and didn't teach anything else. I didn't know those songs, and I wanted to read or learn something new.

I nodded. "I don't want to go to another school."

"Oh, shut up. You need to go. Now get out there and do as I told you."

Carmen grumbled and opened the door.

In the center of the town's marketplace, Vati worked at putting up the merry-go-round. Franz held up one of the pictures that was almost as large as he was. His hands pushed against the wooden frame holding the painted canvas, and his small body tensed forward to keep it balanced against the beam in the middle of the merry-go-round. Vati bolted the frame to the beam and to the picture next to it.

Vati had aligned the pack trailer, where we stashed our attractions after each fair, next to our caravan. Now its door gaped wide open, and sunlight streamed into the dark interior. The plywood for the floor of the merry-go-round leaned against its side.

School had let out for the day. We could tell by the small crowd of local children that gathered at a respectful distance and watched Vati and Franz in bright-eyed fascination. Some still carried their satchels on their backs.

I followed Carmen down the caravan's steps. A girl at the edge of the crowd inched away from the other kids and shuffled toward us. A smaller girl and a blond little boy wearing *Lederhosen* followed in her wake. The boy sucked his thumb, his blue eyes wide.

The older girl stopped and stared at us. "Hi," she said.

Her small entourage hid behind her. The little girl peeked from behind her back, eyes wide in wonder.

"Hi," I answered. Carmen stared back, a frown on her face.

"Do you really live in the caravan?" the girl asked, getting bolder.

Carmen sighed. "Where's your school?"

The local girl turned her head, braids flying. She pointed. "Over there."

I couldn't see anything. "Are you going to school tomorrow?" I asked.

"Yes."

"When does it start?" Carmen wanted to know.

The girl took a step back.

I smiled at her. "We have to go to school too. When does it start?"

"At eight." She ignored my smile and stared at me.

Carmen hurried up the steps. She took the last two in one bound and disappeared inside, slamming the caravan door behind her.

"Thanks," I said. I liked that girl, even though she was just a simple village child. With her big, blue eyes, she reminded me of the nurse I had when I was in the hospital for my eye. I stepped closer.

"My name is Sonja. What's yours?"

"Karin." Now she smiled. She pointed to the little girl and boy. "They are my brother and sister. What grade are you in?"

"Fourth. My sister is in sixth, my little sister's in third, and my brother's in first."

"I'm in fourth too. You all coming to school tomorrow?"

"Yes. How do we get to school from here?"

"If you want I can pick you up on my way. I live right over there."

She pointed at the far end of the marketplace to a pretty white house with a wire fence surrounding clumps of irises and tulips. A terra-cotta garden gnome, surrounded by daffodils and proudly wearing his peaked red cap, leaned on a miniature hoe.

We couldn't have gardens. By the time something grew, we'd be long gone. I shook off a sudden touch of sadness and watched Karin's little sister gawk at Vati, who was positioning the wooden floor around the center of the merry-go-round.

Mutti always said not to make friends with the local kids, but I wished I could. They were so excited about our carnival. I wished I could stay and be Karin's friend.

Thursday morning, Mutti woke us early. We washed our hands and faces and found something clean to wear. Mutti fed us slices of rye bread with jam and some milk and gave us each a small paper bag with a sandwich for *grosse Pause* [lunch break] around ten thirty. School usually let out around one, so Mutti waited for us to come home for lunch. She shooed us out of the door at a few minutes to eight.

Karin stood in front of our caravan, not bold enough to knock. We four children filed out.

"Hi," I said to Karin. "Where are your brother and sister?"

Karin fell in step with me. "They're too young to go to school." She looked at me from the corner of her eyes. "Maybe the teacher will let you sit next to me."

Carmen, Josefa, and Franz lagged behind.

School was held in a two-story building wedged between much taller buildings. Inside, a rope across the stairs and a note kept the children away from the upper level. I wondered if a bomb had hit the building during the war. But the war had been so long ago. At least ten years. They should have fixed that by now.

I forgot about the war when I saw the doors of three rooms on the ground floor wide open. Karin showed Carmen and Franz to their rooms, and Josefa and I followed her into ours. "We have two classes in our room," she explained. "The third and fourth."

Karin meandered between the rows of desks to hers in the third row. Josefa and I stepped next to the teacher's desk and stood there, straight and stiff, satchels on our backs, waiting for the teacher and ignoring the stares from the other kids. The local children dribbled in and found their seats behind the small wooden desks. Some ignored us and dug in their satchels, while others stared at us with wide eyes.

"What's your name?" a boy with a runny nose called from the first row. He wiped his nose on his shirtsleeve. Josefa and I ignored him.

My heart pumped harder. I hoped the teacher would be nice and not treat me as if I didn't know anything, as the teacher in the last town had. *Just because I'm from the carnival doesn't mean I'm stupid*, I thought. Maybe I wasn't smart at home. That's why my brother and sisters called me stupid. But in school I almost always knew the answers.

The bell rang, and the teacher, a tall, spare man, entered. He looked stern and forbidding in his white shirt and tweed jacket. The door clanged shut. I jumped because it sounded almost like a shot. My attention returned to the children, who sprang to their feet.

"*Guten Morgen, Herr Lehrer* [Good morning, teacher]," they called in unison. Then they folded their hands and prayed. I also folded my hands, careful not to bend too low so my satchel wouldn't slip on my back. I glanced at Josefa. She had followed my lead.

After the class finished the Lord's Prayer, the teacher took note of us. "Where do you two come from?"

I answered. "We're from the carnival. I'm in the fourth grade; my sister is in the third grade."

"Do you girls know how to pray?"

We had just prayed with the class. He probably wanted to know if we knew the prayer by heart. Next to me, Josefa stared at the teacher with big, brown eyes. She didn't answer. I, as the older one, should answer this question. My heartbeat sped up, and I mumbled the Lord's Prayer.

I didn't connect the prayers in school with the prayers I said in my heart at home. In my mind, praying in school was more like saying a short poem. I thought people only prayed in school because they were supposed to. I was sure no one ever prayed at home like I did.

The teacher's next question brought me back from my thoughts about prayer.

"Do you know your ABCs?"

I nudged Josefa. That was second grade stuff. Josefa knew how to do that. She looked at me and rattled off the alphabet.

"Okay then. You can sit in the last row." He guided us down the aisle to the back of the classroom.

I squeezed by Karin's desk. She smiled at me. I smiled back. At least I'd already made a friend.

The teacher told me to take off my satchel and sit at an empty desk next to a blonde girl with colorless eyelashes. Josefa waited behind him.

He turned to me. "Do you two know how to read?"

"We do, but we don't have any books. Can we have books?"

"No, you leave again next week, right? No sense giving you books for such a short time."

He turned to Josefa. "You can sit with Fritz here. Fritz, share your book." The teacher looked back at me and added, "Bertha will share her books with you."

Bertha pushed her open book at me. Her eyes never left my face.

The teacher returned to the front of the room and assigned a chapter from the book to be read out loud. Bertha read the first paragraph and held the book out to me.

The teacher leaned against his desk, watching me.

I turned to the page and fluently read the next paragraph, half delighted at my ability and half angry at the teacher's look. He probably thought I had lied to him.

After the reading, the teacher told the children to take out a piece of paper and their colored pencils. He wanted them to draw a picture of last year's merry-go-round, since it was carnival week. I twiddled with my red pencil, stared out the window behind Bertha, and watched the large linden tree in the schoolyard. I had drawn different attractions in the last three schools I attended. A bird landed on the tree and disappeared between the leaves. Maybe I could draw a bird.

All around me the children whispered excitedly as they looked over each other's shoulders and compared drawings. Bertha shyly showed me her picture and asked if it was like our merry-go-round.

I inspected it and nodded. "It's good."

For *grosse Pause*, we went into the schoolyard and ate our sandwiches. Josefa and I stayed close together. Soon we found Carmen and Franz, and before we finished our sandwiches, a crowd had gathered around us. Now the local children were less shy, and their questions came fast.

"Where are you from?"

"Can you ride the merry-go-round for free?"

"Do you know how to play hopscotch?"

Carmen swallowed the rest of her sandwich and nodded to the last question, which an older girl had asked.

"Come on, let's play," the girl said and pulled on Carmen's and my hands. A crowd of girls surrounded us, ready to play. Josefa wandered over to the swings, and Franz drifted toward the smaller boys.

After the lunch break, the children practiced a song they would sing for the mayor during the carnival festivities. In the last hour, they practiced a special dance. We didn't get any homework. In the last school we went to, the teacher had also said since it was carnival time no one had to do homework.

After school on Thursday, we three girls set up the shooting gallery. We carried the beams from the pack trailer and placed them on the spot

Vati designated. Josefa held the corner beam upright, and I aligned the back beam to it. Carmen knelt on the cobblestones and bolted them together. We did the same with the other side and bolted the corrugated sheet metal backing onto the beams. Pockmarks, where the shots from the air guns hit, dented the green paint on the sheet metal. When we finished, Vati put the canvas on the roof, and we fastened it to the sides.

A crowd of school children gathered close, watching. Karin lingered in the back of the crowd, smiling at me when I looked up. One of the older girls Carmen had played with at school approached and asked if she could help.

Carmen frowned and tightened the rope holding the roof to the side. "No, locals aren't allowed to help."

"I need to get home, anyway." The girl left. Some of the other kids followed her, but a few remained and stared at us. The image of a tiger in a cage, powerless to keep everyone from staring, flashed through my mind. I almost understood how that tiger felt.

On Friday, the classroom resounded with whispers. The children couldn't sit still. Everybody stared at us carnival kids during lessons, and at recess everyone wanted to be our friends. Invariably, my new friends asked for free merry-go-round tickets, but Vati always said I wasn't supposed to give them any.

The feeling that the other children regarded me as they would some strange being from darkest Africa never left me. I wasn't like the other children, and under normal circumstances they would never have accepted me. But on Fridays I had many friends.

Saturday school let out after just a few hours, at eleven. We hurried home, ate a quick lunch, and helped Vati open the attractions.

On Monday, the principal had canceled school due to the festival, but Karin came by in the early afternoon, and we wandered the fairgrounds together, talking about the differences in our lives.

16

TRAVEL DAYS

I HOLD A BLACK-AND-WHITE PHOTO OF VATI'S MERRY-GO-ROUND, YEL-
lowed with age. The houses in the background look ancient and
picturesque with their dark beams in white stucco. The town seems
prosperous, despite the ravages of the war.

I look up and study Mutti's wrinkled face. I still see the lovely young
woman who raised me from a child to adulthood. "I don't remember
seeing much of the devastation of the war when I was a child. I remember
bombed-out houses when I was really small, after the orphanage, but later
everything looked whole."

Mutti spreads her gnarled hands. "That's one of the reasons we ran
the carnival in the small villages. Don't get me wrong. I'm a city girl and
will prefer the city for the rest of my life. But after the war the farm-

ers were so much better
off than the people in the
cities. They had money
and food and were hardly
touched by the war, espe-
cially in Hessen, the center
of Germany. That's why we
decided to make our living
in that area."

MERRY-GO-ROUND

I nod. I remember those
small villages well. And I

remember traveling, when everything seemed to be on hold until we arrived in the next town.

SUMMER 1957

Tuesday morning dawned upon a deserted and littered carnival ground. I stepped from our caravan into the early sunlight. A breeze stirred the chilly air, but the cloudless sky promised a warm day later on. On my way to school, I surveyed the aftermath of the festivities. Our attractions hunkered on the littered cobblestones of the town's marketplace, looking like prehistoric animals, covered in green-and-gray-striped canvas. The fair tent, on the distant side of the marketplace, smelled like old beer and sausage gone bad, even from here.

I marched to school with Karin and my siblings. Vati would dismantle the attractions and load them into our pack trailer while we attended school.

At school, the children squirmed in their seats, still excited from the festivities. The teacher, in a mellow mood, and maybe still feeling the effects of the night before, praised the class for their good singing and dancing. Eventually he got around to having us read a few pages about Martin Luther in a history book. Later we worked on two pages of multiplication problems. At the end of class, the teacher gave a few math problems for homework, but we carnival kids didn't have any books, and tomorrow would be our last school day there anyway.

I walked back with Karin, promising we'd return the next year. At the caravan, Carmen told Mutti we didn't have any homework. Mutti shrugged and said, "Okay."

Vati had already dismantled the shooting gallery and stashed it in the pack trailer. The center of the merry-go-round, without the pictures to cover the innards, displayed the simple electrical motor that ran it, nestled between struts and cables. Vati stood on the ladder and removed the last few pictures from the roof.

The winter before, he had painted the pictures for our merry-go-round. Now he took another picture down the ladder to the pack trailer and pushed it in on its wooden frame, the painted canvas buffered and protected with rags.

By dusk, he had also packed the merry-go-round, and the pack wagon stood tightly shuttered and ready to go. We were done here and would move on.

As it so often would, a vague hope settled in my heart. Soon we would be in a new place. Maybe it would be different. Maybe I would find a real friend or we'd stay longer than just a few days. I thought of Karin. She would have made a good friend. Too bad we had to go.

At dinner Vati declared we would leave the next day, as soon as he returned from hauling the pack trailer to the next town. It would be late, but he wanted to leave anyway so we'd arrive early on Thursday.

"Does that mean we have to stay the night along the road again?" Mutti asked. She sighed. "I hate that."

"Yes. I'm sorry you don't like it, but I won't have the attractions up in time otherwise."

I smiled. Staying alongside a road meant we'd be out in the country somewhere, all by ourselves. No new town to get used to, and no new school for a day. I wondered what the place where we'd stay overnight would look like.

In the morning, Vati started the tractor and backed it toward the pack trailer's hitch. He sat high on the tractor and yelled for Mutti. After a quick warning for us to stay inside, she hurried out, guided the hitch into place, and made sure the pack trailer was well secured to the tractor. She stepped back and waved him on. Vati waved back and eased the tractor and pack trailer from the carnival grounds. Once on the street, he accelerated all the way to the thirty-five kilometers our Deutz tractor could handle and disappeared around the corner toward the next town.

By about three that afternoon, the rumbling *tuck, tuck, tuck* of the tractor announced Vati's return. He ate his late lunch, fried potatoes with bacon and egg, which Mutti had ready for him.

Vati lit his after-lunch cigarette and warned us to hurry and secure everything. He would be ready to leave in half an hour. He took a drag of the cigarette and went outside to disconnect the electricity.

With some bickering about who had to wash and who could dry, Carmen and I washed the dishes. Mutti yelled for us to be quiet and to hurry. We finished the dishes and put them away. Mutti stuffed sofa pillows on top to protect them and locked the cabinet doors. She lugged the radio into Eva's bed and covered it with a feather quilt.

It was my turn to empty the slush bucket. I locked the toy drawer instead and dawdled around. Carmen stuck her tongue out at me and hauled the almost-empty fresh water bucket outside to empty it, so the water wouldn't spill out during the trip.

Mutti noticed the still-full slush bucket and glared at me. "Sonja, now!"

I knew what she meant and lugged the odorous bucket outside toward a weedy corner, where I upended it.

Vati started the tractor again, a sure sign he was ready to leave. Mutti pushed me out of the way to check the drawers in the living room and make sure nothing would break during the trip.

A bump shivered through the caravan, and we were connected.

"Where's Wally?" I yelled. I searched behind the cold stove and under the coffee table. She wasn't in the caravan. Carmen ran outside and called her name.

"Wally! Wally, come here!" she called, searching under the caravan and in the weedy ditches. No Wally.

Carmen returned. "I can't find her," she said, almost yelling. "We can't leave without her."

Another bump, this time in front of our caravan. Vati had unhinged the steps to the front door. He carried them to the back of the caravan, where he hooked them into the slats on the wall. The tractor rumbled, and our home trembled and quaked in rhythm to the noise.

Vati opened the front door and announced, "I'm leaving now."

"You can't. Wally isn't here," we children yelled.

At that moment, a whine announced our dog. Vati bent and scooped her up.

"Here she is," he said. Wally jumped from his arms into the caravan, claws scratching the linoleum on the kitchen floor. She must have heard the tractor and knew she needed to hurry home, or she might be left behind.

"Are you ready?" Vati asked one last time.

"Yes," we chimed in unison.

Vati helped Mutti jump from the caravan.

"Eva, you come with me in the car," Mutti said.

"Okay," Eva said and grabbed her doll.

Mutti helped her down from the caravan. She admonished Carmen one last time to make sure to keep the caravan door locked so no one would fall out. Vati connected the VW with a tow bar under the caravan door. Mutti would steer the VW with the gears in neutral.

Josefa, who watched Eva climb into the VW, called after Vati. "Can I ride with you on the tractor?"

"Not now. Maybe the next time." He turned toward our brother. "Franz, you're coming with me on the tractor."

Franz made a face at Josefa. Josefa turned her back to him and marched into the living room. Carmen already sat on the sofa, an open book in her lap.

I ensconced myself on the screwed-down bus seat in the kitchen, leaned against the wall that separated the kitchen from the living room, and hugged Wally. With my head against the cool window glass, I watched the world go by outside. Vati's tractor chugged ahead, and our carnival caravan rocked gently. My back was toward the tractor, and as Vati pulled the caravan into the street, the view unrolled backward. Josefa joined me, and we counted the passing cars.

My heart grew lighter when I spied a small shrine along the roadside, a statue of Mary and Jesus decorated with a jar of wildflowers. We were moving into an area where people believed in God and Jesus.

We passed a stone crucifix, and I felt vaguely guilty. I was sorry for Jesus and wished he didn't have to suffer for me. On the other hand, I was glad he loved me and took away my sins with his suffering.

Josefa spied another car passing the caravan, and I joined her in counting.

When dusk fell, Vati veered off the road into a weedy place. He parked the caravan and left the tractor connected so he could start driving again early in the morning.

Mutti put the radio back into the living room so Eva had a place to sleep and unlocked the food closet.

She allowed us to go outside. "But stay in sight," she called after us. "Just in case."

She didn't say in case of what.

I explored the weedy spot along the rutted path. A small creek with a crop of wild peppermint along the bank invited me to skip a few stones. I picked a handful of peppermint, and Mutti stored it in a bag in the cupboard to make peppermint tea when we arrived at our next destination.

That evening, we ate sandwiches in the gathering dusk. Mutti lit a candle in the living room and pulled out the chessboard from under the sofa bed. She told us to stay in the kitchen, lit another candle on the kitchen table, and gave us an old set of playing cards.

Shadows danced on the brown walls every time we put down a card. Carmen held up her hand and moved her pointy fingers just right. A shadowy dog with long ears took shape against the kitchen wall. When she saw it, Wally barked at it and wagged her tail. Josefa made a shadow bird, and I did a swan. When Mutti sent us to bed, she said we didn't have to wash because it was too dark to go to the creek, and we had only drinking water until we arrived at our destination.

I woke to the swaying of our home and the soothing rumble of the tractor's engine. Without waking us, Vati had gotten up early and pulled onto the road. I snuggled deeper into my feather quilt, lulled by the sound and motion. I was at home, even out here. Safety and peace surrounded me.

One by one, my siblings woke. We stayed in bed, talking and listening to the sound of the tractor. When our stomachs started growling, we rose and got dressed in our wobbly world, wondering when we would get to the new town and have breakfast.

We arrived in the town a little later. Vati unhitched the car and the tow bar, reattached the stairs, and left for the town hall to get permission to hook into the electricity on the fairgrounds. When he returned, he connected the power.

Mutti inspected her meager possessions to make sure everything had survived once again. She told Carmen to get the canister and find water, while the rest of us put everything back into its place. Josefa unlocked the cabinets, and I replaced the pillows on the sofa.

Carmen returned with a full canister and said we could get our water from the public well near the marketplace, not too far into town.

When everything returned to normal, Mutti sent me to find a bakery and get fresh buns, and finally we had breakfast.

After breakfast, Mutti sent us out to find our next school. We had arrived in another town, to get ready for another fair.

17

MARTIN

WHEN I LEFT TO JOIN THE CIRCUS," MUTTI SAYS, "I THOUGHT I was doing something romantic and heroic. And I had so much fun!"

She sighs and takes another swallow of her morning coffee. "But after your Vati sold the circus, the carnival was a step down. By then, the glamour of the traveling life had worn off. It was impossible for it not to. I had five children all crowded into a tiny caravan, took care of all the household chores, and on the weekends I worked, besides making sure you children were all right."

I remember. Mutti seemed harried and short-tempered on the weekends. "The *Racklos* [hired workers] helped Vati. Did having them make your life any easier?"

"Not really," Mutti answers. "We could hardly afford to pay them, so we got some of the lowest of the low to help us. We couldn't trust them alone in the shooting gallery, so they mainly helped Vati. I still had to do all my work, and I had to cook for them too."

"I thought Martin was really nice."

"Who was Martin?"

"He was our first *Racklo*."

"Oh."

Mutti doesn't seem to remember him, but I will never forget Martin.

SUMMER 1958

"*Essen kommen* [Come, eat]," Mutti called through the caravan's open door.

Vati put down the screwdriver he was using to tighten the seats on the merry-go-round and clumped up the five steps into the kitchen.

I sat between Carmen and Josefa on the bus seat in the kitchen. A dark shape ducked through the door after Vati. I quit playing with my spoon and stared at the stranger who had entered our home. He was a brown-eyed, curly-haired older man. At least eighteen to my nine years, he seemed almost as old as my Vati.

Vati introduced him as Martin.

"Martin will help us with the attractions," Vati declared. "I built an apartment for him in the back of the pack trailer, but he'll eat with us from now on."

Vati sat in his chair opposite me, but Martin stood by the door, turning his hat in his large hands.

"Put your hat here." Mutti pointed to the coat hangers by the door. She pulled the kitchen stool from the corner by the sliding door and squeezed it between little Eva's and Franz's chairs, on the short side of the table. Martin sat, making sure to leave room for both children.

The eight plates and their accompanying silverware were so crowded on the table that they almost touched. The space in the center of the table was too small for the pot of mashed potatoes, so Mutti left it on the stove. She took Vati's plate, turned, and spooned a scoop of mashed potatoes onto it, plopped a pork chop next to it, and finished with a few spoonfuls of green beans. She handed Vati the plate and took Martin's next. While she repeated the process, Vati dug in. I fiddled with the silverware and waited my turn.

Mutti cut a pork chop into four parts for us four children. Martin stared at his plate and glanced at Vati, and while Mutti ladled food onto our plates, he folded his hands, closed his eyes, and bowed his head. His lips moved. A moment later, he looked up again. I watched Mutti. Her lips tightened, and a disdainful smile hushed across her face. Martin waited until Mutti sat down with her food before he started to eat.

I hardly tasted my food. I was amazed. Other people prayed too—just like me. From that moment on I loved Martin.

* * *

One evening, I played hide-and-seek with my siblings. Martin worked on the merry-go-round, tightening a screw on the small fence that separated the merry-go-round from the crowds.

Carmen got tired of playing. She'd been "it" for the third time in a row. She said, "I'm going in. I want to listen to the radio."

Josefa and Franz trailed after her. I sat on the merry-go-round steps a few more minutes. Martin finished his job and sat next to me. "What a lovely evening," he said.

I nodded. I wondered if he'd get mad if I asked him something. Mutti would get mad. She didn't want me to talk to Martin. Maybe I should just go in and not say anything. But my feeling of solidarity with Martin, who prayed before eating, was strong. He probably wouldn't mind.

"Why do you pray before you eat?" I asked.

Martin poked the grass in front of the merry-go-round with the tip of his shoe. "Because that's how you show God you're thankful for everything he has given you."

"Is it okay not to pray when your Mutti doesn't want you to?"

"I guess it is. God knows you want to pray even if you can't. I'm sure that makes him happy."

I thought about what I did to make God happy. "I think it makes him happy too when you go to church before Vati opens the business on Sundays."

The Sunday before, when I drifted into the church across from the marketplace where we held the carnival, I had seen Martin already in a pew.

"I'm sure it does. God loves me, and he loves you."

"I go to church too sometimes," I said.

Martin smiled and nodded.

The setting sun painted the sky a lovely orange behind our caravan, and the grass under my feet looked bright green. Martin approved of me. I opened my mouth to tell Martin that it was okay to go to church. I wanted to reassure myself more than him with that remark, but at that moment, the caravan's door opened, and Mutti called. "Sonja, come in."

I rose. Martin did too.

"See you tomorrow," I said.

Martin strode off to his small room at the end of the pack wagon, and I hurried to our home.

"You know better than to talk to the hired help," Mutti said as I came in. "You're the daughter of his boss. Behave like it."

I nodded. But in my heart I knew I'd talk to Martin again, even if he was only hired help.

* * *

Mutti handed me the water bucket. "Go to the faucet and get some water."

I grabbed the bucket and stepped into the dusk. This would be my last trip to the faucet at the edge of the trampled fairgrounds. I placed the bucket under the faucet and turned it on.

"Hello," Martin said.

"Hi, Martin. Aren't you excited? Tomorrow we'll go to winter quarters."

Martin stood next to me, his hands in his pockets. He watched the water splash into the bucket.

"I'm not going with you."

"Why not? Don't you like it with us anymore?"

"I do, but your Vati won't have work for me in the winter, and he won't be able to pay or feed me."

"What will you do, then?"

"I'm going home. Maybe some farmer in the area will hire me."

Suddenly the dusk seemed a lot darker. I watched the water run over the rim of the bucket. "Oh." I turned off the faucet. "I'm sorry you have to go."

Martin held out his hand. A small, dark object lay on his palm. "I have something for you. I whittled it myself during the summer. It's a crucifix."

"For me?" I took the object and inspected it. It was a small wooden cross with a tiny Jesus hanging on it. My heart jumped. I ran my fingers across the image of Jesus, stroking and caressing my treasure.

"So you don't forget God loves you always." Martin smiled and reached out again for a handshake. "You be a good girl, okay?"

"Thank you so much!" I shook his hand, just like an adult.

"I'll carry the bucket." Martin took it and carried it to the front of the caravan with me walking beside him, inspecting my new treasure.

I slipped the crucifix into my pocket, lugged the water up the stairs, and waved at Martin one more time before entering our home.

That night in bed, I turned my new treasure over and over in my hands, tracing the smooth contours of the wood from which Martin had carved it. I knew better than to tell my sisters about it, but maybe I would tell Mutti.

The next morning, Martin knocked on the door. He told Mutti and Vati good-bye and shook their hands, then turned to Carmen, Josefa, and Franz and did the same. When he held out his hand to me, a lump swelled in my throat.

I shook his hand and said good-bye.

"Good-bye," Martin said. He turned, bent down to little Eva, and solemnly shook her hand too. He picked up his duffel bag and strode down the steps of the caravan to the bus stop on the corner, where he disappeared from our lives.

I followed Mutti when she went out to guide the hitch of the pack trailer to connect to the tractor. Vati would be back for us in a few hours, and we'd arrive in our winter quarters before night fell.

After Vati got going, I was alone with Mutti for a rare moment. "Look what Martin gave me." I showed the crucifix to Mutti.

Mutti looked at it, her hands behind her back. She frowned. "That's pretty. It's a nice toy."

"It's a crucifix. It's supposed to remind us of Jesus."

"That Martin put funny ideas in your mind."

I bit my lip. I didn't know what to say.

As I ran back to the caravan, I tried to sort out my mixed emotions. Mutti liked the little present Martin had given me. That made it right for me to have it. But it was a religious present, and that wasn't right. And since Martin was just hired help, a *Racklo*, I probably hadn't behaved as Mutti expected me to, as the boss's daughter, when I took the crucifix.

I hid my small treasure under my mattress and didn't show it to anyone else.

I never saw Martin again, but I never forgot him. His quiet, sure beliefs strengthened my determination to cling to my own faith in God, even at such a young age.

* * *

After Martin, two more *Racklos* worked for us, and then Vati decided we children were old enough to take over the job. He didn't want strange men around his girls.

Nevertheless, strange men abounded in our business, and I'll never forget my encounter with a dangerous stranger when I was ten.

18

IN PERIL

MUTTI AND I MEANDER THROUGH THE PRODUCE SECTION OF THE grocery store, watching Liesel and Meagan, arms around each other, saunter ahead of us, oblivious to the displays of bananas, apples, and onions flanking them.

"They are probably talking about boys," Mutti says, turning a cantaloupe in her hand.

"Actually, they're planning a girls' night with Kathie. They'll stay overnight at her house this weekend."

"How big they are. When you girls got older, Vati and I had to watch out for you all the time. I still remember how often I called you from behind the caravan, away from the local boys."

"It wasn't that often."

Mutti places the cantaloupe into the shopping cart, her mind in the past.

"It was hard in the summers, with my pretty girls at all those carnivals. We were lucky nothing ever happened to you."

Something did, but even now I won't tell her.

SUMMER 1958

That summer, I was going on eleven. One of the women of the small hamlet where we held the carnival came up the steps to the open door of the caravan, calling a greeting. She lugged a large cloth bag behind her.

"Seeing you have children of all ages," she said, "I thought maybe you can use some of these clothes. They're from my kids and grandkids."

Mutti accepted them with a bright smile and thanked her.

After the woman left, Mutti dumped the contents of the bag onto the sofa. White undershirts tangled with green and yellow sweaters, and heavy dark-green and brown cloth announced that boys' pants also hid in the pile. I looked for the brighter colors because they were clothes for us girls. A glimpse of wine red caught my attention. I dug for the red garment, pulled a knitted cardigan from the pile, and held it up. The buttons, the same red as the cardigan, were still all there. How beautiful it was! It looked brand new. I tried it on, and it fit just right. It felt nice and warm too.

Josefa pointed at it. "I want that. I like it."

"You don't need one. Let Sonja have it," Mutti decreed.

I kept it on. Mutti picked out the boy clothes for Franz, put them aside, and decided who would get what.

I noticed a short, straight skirt. It was camelhair brown. I tried it on, and it fit perfectly.

"Looks good on you," Mutti said. "You're starting to look like a woman."

I stood a bit straighter, pushed my chest out, and smiled.

Carmen dropped the blouse she held back onto the pile. "I want it. I'm older and already have a figure."

I stuck my tongue out at her. "You already have a straight skirt, not a figure."

"You're just a kid. Wannabe woman." Carmen stalked off.

I went into the bedroom and admired myself in the mirror Vati had glued to the inside of the door. In my straight skirt, I looked different, almost pretty. I poufed my hair the way Carmen had shown me and put in a new pin. Very nice! I smiled at myself in the mirror. My eyes fastened on my front. Was it real or just my imagination? I pushed out my chest, inspecting it. I thought I had filled out a little. And the tight new skirt showed off my hips. I was almost a woman, all right.

Mutti packed away the clothes, and pretty soon it was time for the carnival to open. I wanted to show off my new look. I put on one of the blouses the woman had given us, tucked it into my new skirt, slipped my new red cardigan over it, and went outside.

Vati unlocked the ticket booth and asked Carmen and me to watch the merry-go-round while he went to get the records from our living room. The record player in the ticket booth was connected to two large loudspeakers, which blasted the music into the fairgrounds. Several packages of record needles hid in the drawer under the record player. They wore out after playing just three or four songs, so Vati always had some spares. At the end of Sunday, the worn-out needles would litter the ground around the ticket booth like exotic silver seeds.

Vati came down the steps, his arms loaded with records. He hurried back to us and the ticket booth. Almost there, he stubbed his toe on a rock and lost his balance. He caught himself before he fell, but the records tumbled off each other one by one and shattered on the cobblestones. Vati stood before the broken shards, half bent over and hands on his knees, staring at the black mess and cussing in Polish. He went to his knees and sifted through the shards. The sun glinted on his thick white hair.

Carmen and I stayed put. We didn't want to risk him yelling at us, since he was already angry.

Finally, he drew one unbroken record from the wreckage. "I'll play that one, then," he muttered, came back to the ticket booth, and put it onto the record player. He looked up and saw us still standing by the open ticket-booth door. He made a shooing gesture with his hand. "Go help Mutti with the shooting gallery."

At the back door of the shooting gallery, Mutti saw us and beckoned for Carmen. "Sonja, I don't need you. You can help Josefa tend Eva in the caravan."

The caravan was empty. Josefa had probably taken Eva out to inspect the local candy stands. I wandered by them but didn't see my sisters. People strolled past me with gleaming eyes and open mouths, taking in the blue and orange paper flowers in the shooting gallery and the assortment of sweet gingerbread hearts with iced decorations in red, yellow, and green. The carnival smell of bratwurst, hot cotton candy, and various other delights drifting from the stands the local businesses had set up wafted through the air.

A line of boys, accompanied by giggly girls in ponytails wearing wide skirts, stood in front of the merry-go-round's ticket booth. Vati had just ended a ride. The chain seats slowed to a stop, and laughing teenagers unhooked their seat belts and jumped from the seats. Others crowded to get an empty seat.

A local girl, walking hand-in-hand with a boy, glanced at me with bright blue eyes and moved on, hips swinging. *I'm just as pretty as that girl*, I thought, *but maybe a little younger. Just a little bit.* I wondered what it would be like to hold a boy's hand.

I walked by the open end of the *Bierzelt* [beer tent] and squinted inside. People pushed by, carrying paper plates covered with potato salad and bratwurst with mustard and sauerkraut. A counter stood to the side of the stage at the narrow end of the tent, behind which barrels of beer released their foaming contents from the taps into large glass mugs. Two men filled the mugs and sold the beer. A crowd around the counter waited for their turn. The yeasty smell of the beer mixed with the odor of food and too many bodies in the close quarters of the tent. I wrinkled my nose and breathed more shallowly.

A band sat on folding chairs on the stage and played their trumpets, tubas, trombones, and horns. One young man undulated in rhythm with his accordion, fingers flying over the buttons. The sound of the "Beer Barrel Polka" filled the tent and spilled out the entrance. People sat close together on the benches, swaying to the rhythm. I stood in the shade of the rolled-back tent flaps and hummed with the band.

I wandered on, checking on Carmen and Mutti in the shooting gallery. They weren't busy yet. I leaned against the counter, talking to Carmen, who encouraged me to shoot one of the flowers to attract customers. She put in the pellets and handed me the gun.

Since I couldn't see out of my right eye, I shot left-handed. I knew the guns and seldom missed, even though I'm not a natural left-hander. Soon a crowd of young men surrounded me, gawking at my skill. Since Carmen and Mutti now had their hands full, I took off, wandering past Vati's merry-go-round and toward one of the candy stands the locals had put up.

A tall, skinny man about my father's age approached me. "I saw you shooting," he said. "You shoot well."

I squinted at him and smiled. Somebody noticed me. I stroked my tight skirt. Maybe he saw how pretty I looked. "It's no big deal."

The man smiled at me. "Could you do me a favor? I'll pay you a five-pfennig piece."

"Sure," I replied. Jesus said to help others. I was happy to help anyone. It made me feel wanted and appreciated.

"Can you buy me a mug of beer?"

"Okay." With the coins he gave me fisted in my hand, I set off for the tent, skipping along. The German version of "Personality" drifted from the merry-go-round. I hummed along, feeling happy and grown up. Here I was, helping someone and even earning a little money.

When I returned, the man still stood by the candy stand. With his hands in his pockets, he stared at the crowds. I held the mug out to him.

He didn't take his hands out of his pockets. "Could you carry it for me? Just to the hill over there?" He took one hand from his pocket and pointed.

"Sure." He'd probably give me the promised five-pfennig piece when we got to the hill.

I carried the mug and marched after him away from the fairgrounds and the town. He went along a small dirt path. Fields of young wheat with light-green heads bobbing in the breeze flanked the path. Wheat and raps fields surrounded the grassy clearing, where we stopped. The man sat on the grass and leaned back. I held out the mug and waited for my coin.

The stranger took the mug, sipped on it, and placed it on the grass. "Sit down," he said. "I want to show you something."

I sat next to him. "Okay. But then I would like my five-pfennig piece."

"You are such a pretty girl." I smiled at the unexpected compliment, but something deep inside recoiled.

"Give me your hand." He grabbed my hand and made me touch him.

His face came closer, much too close. Suddenly everything felt wrong. My body tensed, and I swallowed. I struggled to pull my hand free, but he held on tightly. I searched the empty field for help, but no one was in sight.

My stomach constricted, and the world grew dim. A sense of unreality came over me, as if I were in a dream. I heard a voice deep in my head saying, "Get up and run. Now!"

Again I tried to jerk away my hand, but to no avail. "I have to go," I yelled.

"In a minute." His voice was hoarse.

I wavered. He was an adult, and I obeyed adults. But maybe it was God that had told me to run. I felt like throwing up. I sat there, caught and scared. Then with all my strength, I jerked my hand from his, jumped up, and ran as hard and fast as I could.

I glanced back, afraid he was chasing after me. The man had gotten up and stood there, watching me run away. He slumped his shoulders and looked like someone who felt really bad. I raced to the fairgrounds and our carnival, and I didn't quit running until I yanked open the caravan door and exploded into the safety of our home.

Silence greeted me. I pulled the washbowl from under the stove and ladled water into it. I rubbed soap into my hand and scrubbed until the skin turned pink. After I rinsed, I poured the water outside into the grass. Then I put away all evidence of my activity.

To calm myself, I tried reading, but I couldn't concentrate, so I said a quiet prayer and asked God to forgive me if I had done something wrong. After the prayer, the darkness in my heart eased. It was okay. Jesus loved me still. Maybe I should tell Mutti what had happened, but I was sure she would get mad at me. Right then, I decided to never again buy beer for strange men.

19
A VISIT

UTTI AND I WALK ALONG THE STOREFRONTS IN DOWNTOWN
Provo. We pass by a small school where I taught ESL classes. I
point to the school. "I used to work there, teaching English to
people from different countries."

"I worked many different jobs in my life," Mutti says. "I even worked
as a hotel maid one time."

"When was that?"

"In '59." She's quiet.

1959. I remember that time. I was twelve that summer. It's still difficult for me to think about what happened, let alone talk about it. I
hesitate. "That must have been after Sergey visited."

Mutti nods and points out the new fashions in the store windows.
Like me, she doesn't want to talk about that time. I walk next to her,
admiring the new wares in a small boutique, but my mind is back in 1959,
and the events of that summer unfold in my memory.

SUMMER 1959

Twenty-one divided by three; that's easy. I wrote a seven into the little
square next to the equal sign.

Josefa, beside me on the kitchen bench, sighed and wrote something
on her lined paper. I glanced out the window. Outside, Carmen and
Franz, one on each side, held a large picture to the center beam of the
merry-go-round while Vati screwed it tight.

I wanted to echo Josefa's sigh, but I kept my mouth shut and turned to tackle the next math problem.

A knock sounded on the door.

Mutti, who, in a rare moment of leisure, sat on the sofa, reading one of the doctor novels she liked so much, said, "*Herein* [Come in]."

A tall man opened the door. His wide shoulders obscured the light coming in from outside, and his deep blue eyes glinted. Sparse blond hair grew around his ears, leaving the top of his head bald.

He glanced at us. "Does Margot Francesco live here?"

"It's for you, Mutti," I called.

Mutti looked up from her novel. The book fell from her hand, and her eyes grew big. "Oh my, it's Sergey!"

Sergey grinned and held out his arms. "Margot, is that you?"

Mutti jumped up and flew into his arms. "Sergey! What are you doing here?"

"Hello," I said.

Josefa echoed the greeting. Eva came into the kitchen from the living room, a blue toy car in her hand.

Mutti pushed away from the stranger and turned toward us. "Go on out, children. Go play."

Josefa and I closed our schoolbooks and picked them up to stash into the satchel.

"Leave them on the table," Mutti said. "Just go out. Leave."

We hurried outside. Five-year-old Eva scrambled after us, the toy still in her fist.

I wondered if we should tell the rest of the family about the strange visitor.

Vati had finished the center of the merry-go-round, and now he and Franz dragged a fence section toward it. Carmen swept out the pack trailer. I didn't want to interrupt Vati and make him mad, so I walked to the merry-go-round, checking out the local children who were watching Vati. Josefa followed. Vati screwed the fence section in place and stretched. He took a pack of cigarettes from his breast pocket and tapped one out. He saw me and Josefa. "Are you finished with your homework?" The unlit cigarette dangled from his hand.

I was bursting with curiosity about the strange visitor. Maybe Vati knew who that man was and would tell us. "No," I said. "A man came to visit Mutti and she told us to go outside."

"His name is Sergey," Josefa added.

Vati frowned. The cigarette in his hand broke, and he threw it to the ground. He spat and said something in his native Polish. It sounded like a swear word. Vati strode to our caravan. I stared after him. A funny feeling came over me, and my stomach started to ache. Josefa and I followed Vati at a safe distance. Franz trailed after us.

We stopped by the side of the caravan. Vati stormed up the four steps and pulled open the door. He yelled something in Polish or Russian. The stranger yelled back, but I couldn't make out the words. Vati marched inside and slammed the door shut.

Vati's and Sergey's raised voices pelted through the closed door of the caravan. Between their voices, Mutti's higher voice brought a counterpoint, quieter and more soothing but also in that strange language. Josefa and I moved closer to each other. Franz joined us, and Eva's little hand crept into mine. I held on to her. Carmen finished sweeping the pack trailer, closed it, and joined us.

"They're speaking Russian. They don't want us to know what's happening," she whispered. Nobody answered. We stood, clustered together in silent companionship.

I was still holding Eva's hand when Sergey backed down the stairs, rapidly talking in his strange language, hat clenched in his hand. He squinted into the sunlight. Mutti followed, her mouth open as if she wanted to say something. She saw us and closed her mouth. Sergey waved at her and turned away. With large, quick strides, he hurried from the fairgrounds.

"Margot," Vati called harshly.

Mutti turned and went back in. The door slammed shut after her.

I looked at Josefa. She stared back at me with wide eyes. "Let's go play," she said.

We wandered around the caravan to the tractor, where we joined some of the local children we attended school with that week. Without much enthusiasm, we played a bit of soccer with them. Eva sat in the grass, pushing her small car around in a circle and making car noises. My mind wasn't on our game. I wondered what had happened with Vati and Mutti and the stranger in the caravan. Who was this man who could make Vati so angry?

Soon, I lost interest in the game and wandered off through the nearby streets. I admired the houses with their tidy little lawns, once again wondering what it would be like to live in a real house. One day, I promised myself, I would live in one.

Eventually, I trundled home. Hunger warred with a knot in my stomach, a knot of anxiety I didn't quite understand. Mutti stood by the edge of the kitchen table, cutting slices of bread from a round rye loaf. Josefa's and my schoolbooks still lay on the table, pencils next to them.

Mutti looked up when I came in and said, "Hurry and finish your homework. I need the table for supper."

I sat on the bench and went back to puzzling out the problems for tomorrow's math class.

Supper was strange. I was hungry, but when I took a bite, my stomach seemed to close up. I swallowed the bite with effort and sipped my milk. Eva moved one piece of her sandwich around and around the others, as if it were her toy car, and Josefa played with the breadcrumbs on the table. Vati silently sipped his coffee and chewed on his liverwurst sandwich. Only Franz finished his food.

When I came home from school the next afternoon, Mutti had lunch on the table. We ate potatoes, peas and carrots, and bratwurst. Mutti poked at her peas and hardly ate anything.

Vati went outside after dinner.

Mutti came into the kitchen, glossy black curls framing her lipsticked mouth. She wore her midnight-blue dress and high heels. She grabbed her purse from the counter and turned to us. "Carmen, you and Sonja wash the dishes. I'm going shopping. I'll be back in a while."

Carmen nodded. I stared at Mutti, imagining her walking down the cobblestones to the grocery store, her green shopping net swinging from her hand. A stab of pain went through my heart, though, when she stepped outside and closed the door, leaving the shopping net behind.

Carmen pulled the bowl from under the stove. We argued about who would wash and who would dry and put away. Because Carmen was older, she won. I washed, and she dried.

After we finished, we joined Josefa and Franz in the living room to play old maid and checkers. That day, we didn't fight much and even let Eva push some of the pieces.

Vati came in about suppertime. He looked around the kitchen, then came into the living room, watching us children huddled over the checkerboard. "Where's Mutti?"

Carmen looked up, a red checker piece in her hand. "She went shopping, but she hasn't come back yet."

Eva rose and looked at Vati. "I'm hungry."

Vati's mouth set in a thin line. "Make her a sandwich, and make some for yourselves too." He turned and stomped out. A moment later, we heard the VW start. I looked out the kitchen window and watched Vati drive off.

We ate our sandwiches. Neither Vati nor Mutti returned. We played hide-and-seek among the almost-assembled carnival attractions, always on the lookout for our VW. But it got dark, and neither of our parents had returned.

Eva came out from behind the shooting gallery, where she'd been hiding. A tear streaked down her smudgy cheek. "I don't want to play anymore."

Carmen took Eva by the hand. "Let's go in."

We gathered in the living room and turned on the radio, glad we didn't have to go to bed yet but uneasy and subdued nevertheless.

Eva quit crying and started sucking her thumb. She looked tired. I was wondering if we should send her to bed, when I heard the unmistakable *putt-putt* of our Volkswagen.

We jumped up and rushed to the door. The driver's side door opened, and Vati emerged. A moment later the other door opened, and Mutti came out.

A heavy burden lifted from my small shoulders. Mutti was here. I wondered if she had bought anything. But except for her purse, her hands were empty.

Mutti stalked to the caravan, ignoring Vati, who hurried after her. When she came up the stairs, we rushed as one back into the living room. Nobody said a word, but we all knew what to do. We crowded together on the sofa and listened to the music from the radio, as if this were an ordinary evening.

Mutti stormed in. She glanced at us sitting on the sofa and said, "Children, go to bed." She turned to the kitchen table and cleared it of our sandwich plates and wiped the crumbs off the table. We stood in line in the kitchen, waiting our turns to wash our hands and faces.

Mutti glared at us. "Just go to bed. You can wash in the morning."

Vati squeezed by us into the living room, turned the radio off, and sat on the sofa.

Eva started crying again, but Carmen hushed her and helped her into her nightgown.

Before I was even in bed, Vati's deep voice came through the closed door. "What were you thinking of, meeting him like that? Didn't you consider the children?"

I snuggled deeper into my feather quilt and screwed my eyes shut. But sleep didn't come. I tried to think of Jesus, but I couldn't keep out the words coming through the closed door of the living room.

Dear Jesus, please make them quit fighting, I prayed. But even my prayers didn't make my parents' hurtful words go away.

Mutti said, "I told you already. I didn't do anything. We just talked. Since when do you forbid me to meet old friends and talk about my youth? I have a life too."

I wondered what she meant by that. We all had a life together, a carnival life.

Vati's voice rose. "Not with Sergey, you don't. I won't stand for it."

Mutti's voice too went up. "I'm tired of you. I'm tired of being cooped up with the kids every minute of my life. I want out."

I covered my ears with my quilt and rolled onto my side, but I couldn't keep out Mutti's words.

She was tired of us. I always knew I wasn't a good child, and what she just said proved it.

Maybe if I'd change my ways and be perfect from now on, she'd not be tired of us. But I had no clear idea of how to accomplish that. How could I be perfect? I swore to myself that I'd never again fight with my sisters and brother and that I would always immediately do what she wanted me to. Surely then she would be happy living with us.

Finally, I drifted off to sleep.

20

SERGEY

MUTTI TELLS ME HOW MUCH NICER THE STORES ARE IN STUTT-gart, Germany, where she lives. I half listen while she compares Stuttgart to Salt Lake City. She tells me how much bigger, more cosmopolitan, and more beautiful Stuttgart is, but my mind is stuck back in 1959, when my siblings and I were motherless.

I now understand the pressure and stress Mutti was under when we were small. How can I judge what she did so long ago? I have never been in a similar situation and don't know what I would have done.

Even as a twelve-year-old girl, I didn't judge. I just wanted my Mutti back.

SUMMER 1959

That Friday afternoon, Mutti and Carmen went to open the shooting gallery. A few teenagers, the boys in black leather jackets and the girls in tight pink and pastel sweaters, ambled between the attractions but didn't stop to shoot for the prizes. Josefa, Eva, and I sat on the caravan steps. The sun peeked through the cloud cover and warmed my back. I watched the happy and excited teens, my heart heavy. Their laughter mingled with a polka coming from the merry-go-round. They sounded as if they didn't have a care in the world.

My attention returned to the shooting gallery. Carmen collected money from a customer and handed him a rifle. At the other end, a man leaned against the counter. For a moment I didn't recognize him, but then

I realized it was Sergey. Mutti stood close to him inside the shooting gallery, smiling, her gaze focused on his face.

Sergey and Mutti were talking. Every time Mutti smiled at him, a stab of pain knifed through my insides. This stranger had no business with us. Why couldn't he just go away? Didn't he have his own family?

At the merry-go-round, Vati sat in his little booth, starting and stopping the ride and selling tickets in between. At least he didn't notice Sergey and go pick another fight.

I watched Mutti and Sergey and returned to my brooding. What if Mutti liked Sergey better than us? She just might, considering what bad children we were. She always told us how we got on her nerves, and when she was in a really bad mood, she called us names. Her birthday had been two weeks ago, and when I asked Mutti what she wanted, she said she wanted good children. There was no help for it; I wasn't the good child she wanted.

Sergey strode off, a big smile on his face. Mutti picked up a rifle and handed it to an older man, who stood waiting.

Sergey was gone. A heavy weight rolled off my back. Maybe we'd never see him again. I sighed, rose to my feet, and went to the merry-go-round to check on Vati.

Vati beckoned me from the little booth where he sold tickets and controlled the rides. I hurried closer. "Sonja, make me a cup of coffee. You know how I like it."

I waved at Josefa and Eva and skipped home, forgetting about Sergey. I was good at making coffee. Vati often said his coffee tasted best when I made it. He didn't want any of the other kids to do it, just me. I finished brewing it, and, with a big smile, I carried the large, hot cup to the merry-go-round.

The next day, Saturday, Mutti helped Carmen open the shooting gallery, then left her to handle the sparse business of the morning and returned to the caravan. I trailed after her.

She got out a pot and set water to boil for chicken noodle soup. Around noon, Mutti called us in for a lunch of soup and bread, and then she relieved Carmen in the shooting gallery. After Carmen ate, she returned to the shooting gallery. It was my turn to dry the dishes and Josefa's turn to wash.

I was wiping the last cup when Mutti returned, grabbed her purse from the counter, and said, "Sonja, go to the shooting gallery and help

Carmen. Josefa, you watch Eva. Franz, stay with the merry-go-round and Vati. I'll be gone for a little while, so I want you all to be obedient, hear?"

I almost dropped the cup in my hand. This wasn't good. Surely she wasn't going to see Sergey. We probably had run out of butter or sugar, and she was going to the store to get some. But my knees shook, and my stomach roiled. We had enough sugar. Besides, it was Saturday, and the stores were about to close for the weekend.

Mutti left. I pushed the cup into the cupboard, slammed it shut, and slipped out after her. Sick to my stomach, I wandered over the trampled grass of the fairgrounds toward the shooting gallery. From the corner of my eye, I watched Mutti. Dressed in her nice skirt and blouse and carrying her purse, she strode from the fairgrounds toward downtown. She never looked back.

I went around the shooting gallery and entered through the small side door. Once more, from across the counter, I searched for Mutti. Maybe she had changed her mind and returned. But she was gone.

A gaggle of teens gathered around the counter. Among laughs and shouts, they clamored for the guns and held out their money. I focused on selling shots. But my thoughts wandered. Every time I thought of Mutti, my stomach flip-flopped. I wanted to join the misty afternoon rain. I'd feel better sitting in the cold and wet and letting the drizzle wash away the misery in my heart.

As the afternoon wore on, business picked up. Without a break, Carmen and I sold shots and passed out prizes to winning shooters. Before I knew it, darkness fell.

Vati turned on the merry-go-round lights. Colored lightbulbs framed the Mickey Mouse pictures attached to it and punctuated the gathering darkness with drops of red, blue, and orange. The pictures, fascinating in their suddenly red- and blue-tinted frames, whirled around and around.

The flashes of colored light joined the dazzling, hot white lights from the food and candy booths on both sides of the merry-go-round. They spilled over the wandering crowds and lit up a red-lipsticked mouth here and a pair of glittering eyes there.

I searched through the festive darkness. I didn't think Mutti was back, but, I tried to reassure myself, maybe I had missed her return. We had been so busy, after all.

When the stream of younger children wanting rides thinned out, Vati turned the lights off on the merry-go-round, loosed the canvas on the top, rolled it down, and secured it on the bottom.

I was loading an air rifle for a teenager who wanted to impress his girlfriend when Vati came in the back door. He turned to me.

"Where's Mutti?"

"I don't know. She left after lunch and hasn't come back."

Vati took the air gun from me. "Go to bed," he said.

I hurried home. Little Eva and Franz were already in bed, and Josefa was washing her hands and face in the bowl on the kitchen table.

Everything seemed dark and lonely even though my sisters and brother were there and the electric lightbulbs on the ceiling lit the inside of the caravan. Josefa and I went to bed without talking.

I woke up to the familiar smell of coffee and cigarettes. While I climbed out of bed and hurried into my clothes, I prayed in my heart, *Please, dear God, let her be back. Please, let her be back.*

I stood in front of the bedroom door for a moment. I didn't dare open it for fear of being disappointed. Finally I pushed the door handle and opened the door. The sofa bed was folded away, and Vati sat on the sofa, a scowl on his face and smoking his morning cigarette. The smell of coffee wafted from the kitchen. I tiptoed through the living room. My heart raced like a runaway car, and my knees shook. Surely Mutti would be in the kitchen, I told myself, but it didn't help. I was afraid to look.

21

I WANT MY MUTTI BACK!

YOU NEED TO VISIT ME IN STUTTGART," MUTTI SAYS, TEARING ME away from my painful memories. "It's so nice there. We'll go to the opera, like I used to when I was young."

"I was only twelve when you left in 1959. I never saw an opera or anything like that." I'm not able to keep the anger out of my voice. "I saw only small-town carnivals and the caravan. I wish it had been different."

"Don't think my life was all roses. When I was thirteen, Hitler and the Nazi party seized power in Germany. My mother had a new little girl, blonde and blue-eyed. I was inferior. You have no idea what that meant."

I make an effort to understand what Mutti is talking about. "That must have been hard for you."

Mutti finds a bench and sits. "I will never forget the day I went to school and the teacher said all Jewish children could leave early. He told the German children to stay, to learn something new."

"What happened?"

Mutti relates that the teacher allowed her to stay when she asked, since she was both German and Jewish. Then, she went on, he told the Aryan children not to be friends with the Jews. If they'd fall in love with a Jew, their children would be ugly and retarded.

"I was so embarrassed because my mother had fallen in love with a Jew and had me. I ran home and inspected myself in the mirror to make sure I wasn't ugly."

A sudden wave of sympathy for a lonely, unloved little girl engulfs me. Like me, my mother lived through a deeply disturbing experience when she was young. But unlike me, she had no one to talk to about it, not even God.

We leave the bench and decide to return home. Neither of us says much on the way to the light rail, and again my thoughts return to the time when Mutti had left us.

SUMMER 1959

That morning, hoping and praying my Mutti had come home, I finally slipped from the living room into the kitchen. I looked around. The heaviness in my heart lifted. I sighed a big thank you to God.

She was there! Mutti stood at the table, buttering fresh buns. It seemed she had never gone.

Suddenly I was ravenous. The look and smell of the fresh buns and the coffee brewing permeated my small body, and saliva gathered in my mouth. I swallowed and sat at the kitchen table, ready for a bun and some milk. Everything was all right with the world. Mutti was back.

Mutti didn't acknowledge me or Carmen, who had followed me from the bedroom. She took her coffee cup with her into the living room and sat on the sofa at the opposite end from Vati. She glared at him. "I've had enough of your jealousy. I want a life of my own."

Vati slammed his cup onto the saucer on the coffee table. Coffee sloshed over the rim and collected in the saucer. "Go ahead. Do what you want. I won't come after you."

Vati rose and stormed from the caravan. Our small home shook from his steps. One of the violins on the wall twanged. Franz, who had come from the bedroom a minute earlier, grabbed a bun from the kitchen table and hurried after Vati.

Mutti rose and followed them. I sat at the kitchen table with my sisters, forgetting to chew. My hands curled into fists, and something in the air made it hard to breathe. I tried to reassure myself. Surely God hadn't fulfilled my wish and let Mutti come back just so that she would leave again. It couldn't be! Mutti must have changed her mind and followed Vati to tell him so.

But a moment later, she returned with an old suitcase she had taken from the storage boxes perched between the rubber wheels under the caravan.

Tears leaked from my eyes. I couldn't swallow the last bite of my bun.

I wiped my eyes and pressed my hand to my belly.

As one, we girls rose and stood by the living room door, watching Mutti.

Mutti opened the drawers over the bedroom door in the living room, where she stashed her clothes, pulled them out, stuffed them inside the suitcase, and snapped it shut.

"Don't go, Mutti," Carmen ventured.

"We'll be good," I pleaded.

Eva, still in her nightgown, cried and hung on to my hand.

"I'm sorry." Mutti kissed Eva on the cheek. Her eyes held a faraway look, as if she were already gone. With the suitcase in one hand and her purse in the other, she marched through the kitchen. She switched the purse to her shoulder, opened the door, stepped outside, and slammed the door shut behind her.

Carmen ran after her, and the rest of us trailed in her wake. Mutti didn't turn to look at us. She rounded a corner and vanished from our sight. Carmen ran to the merry-go-round to talk to Vati, pulling on his sleeve. Eva, Josefa, and I stood in a knot by the caravan, heads bent. I hugged myself. Eva sucked her thumb, and Josefa played with a strand of her hair. I looked up at Carmen and Vati.

Vati stared in the direction Mutti had disappeared. His shoulders sagged, and then he straightened and hurried to the caravan. We girls trailed after him. Vati shut the door after himself, leaving us outside. A moment later, the door opened again. Vati stepped out onto the top step and left the door wide open.

He looked over our small carnival and turned to us. "Carmen, make lunch and supper and take care of the caravan. Sonja, you watch the younger kids. Don't let Eva out of your sight."

"What about the shooting gallery?" Carmen asked.

"Never mind. You just take care of what I told you."

"When is Mutti coming back?" Franz asked, for once not tough and manly, but somehow diminished and small, like a scared little boy.

"I don't know. Don't worry, she'll be back," Vati said and hurried to the merry-go-round. "Franz, Josefa, come help me." Together they rolled up the canvas around the merry-go-round and got things ready to go.

Vati kept the shooting gallery closed that day. Carmen made us sandwiches for lunch and dinner. After lunch, I put Eva down for a nap. Josefa sat on the sofa in the living room, coloring on an old piece of paper. I decided they would be all right alone for a while. I needed to be by myself.

I wandered down the strange streets away from the fairgrounds, look-ing for Mutti, but I couldn't find her.

Nobody cared whether I was dead or alive. Maybe no one would notice if I left and didn't come back. Vati would be happy. He would have one fewer worry and one fewer mouth to feed.

But Vati had told me to watch the other children, and I wasn't doing my duty. He would be mad if he found out. I decided I'd better return to the caravan.

When I stepped through the narrow caravan door, Carmen was argu-ing with Josefa, trying to get her to wash the dishes. I left again, crawled under the caravan, between the rubber tires, and wedged myself into the middle of the cellar boxes, the same boxes that had held Mutti's suitcase.

Tucked away in my hiding place and in my loneliness, I prayed to God, in whom I had believed for so many years. I promised to be good, to be the perfect child that Mutti wanted, if He'd just send her back. I didn't know how life could go on without her.

I was hugging my knees when a wet nose and a small, inquiring yelp announced that Wally had found me. She snuggled tightly against me and licked my face. I hugged her, glad to have someone who sympathized. Wally understood. Maybe God sent her to comfort me.

Monday morning, with an unreasonable hope in my heart that Mutti would be back, I rose early and hurried into the living room. But Vati lay on the sofa bed alone. No noise or coffee smell came from the kitchen. Nevertheless, hoping I was wrong, I checked. The kitchen was empty. Vati woke and told me to make coffee.

That afternoon, Carmen and I ran the shooting gallery while Josefa took care of Eva and brought us some sandwiches for supper. After dark, when families with smaller children left, Vati closed the merry-go-round, sent Carmen and me to bed, and took over the shooting gallery.

I tagged after Carmen toward the caravan. Maybe Carmen knew when Mutti would return. I watched her stride along, her back stiff and straight, and decided to say nothing. She'd yell at me or call me names if I asked her. And Josefa was younger than I was. She didn't know anything.

Inside, Wally greeted us. I bent and picked her up. She wagged her tail and licked my face.

Tuesday, Vati took down the attractions, and the next day we left the town. Everything went on the same, except without Mutti.

We children were quiet and didn't fight like usual. But neither did we talk about Mutti. Mutti's absence was like a deep, open wound that would hurt more if we picked at it, so we followed our father's example and left it alone. We tried hard to do everything Vati told us to do. Somehow even when the sun shone, things were dark and quiet. Nobody cared to listen to the radio, and we all went to bed in the evenings, if not gladly, at least without protest.

In the next town, we helped Vati put up the attractions.

Friday morning, Vati came into the kitchen, where we were eating our breakfast rolls. "I'm going to call your Tante Brigitte. I'll be back before we have to start the attractions."

"Is Mutti living with her?" Franz asked.

"Yes." Vati opened the door and closed it after him. The steps creaked, and our caravan gave its usual small shudder as he went down them.

"If she's with Brigitte, she'll be back soon," Carmen said.

"Yes, she'll be back soon," Eva echoed.

When Vati returned, we surrounded him.

"Is Mutti all right?"

"Did you talk to her?"

"Is she coming back?"

We all talked at the same time. Vati turned his back to us and shook his head.

"Carmen, cook us some soup for lunch," he said. "Franz and Sonja, help me put the pictures on the merry-go-round. Josefa, play with Eva."

Our eager questions were cut off. Quietly, without fighting, we turned to our tasks. Eva started crying again. I tagged after Vati.

For two more lonely weeks, we carried on by ourselves. Finally, Vati went to call Brigitte once more. When he returned, he told us to be good. He was going to be gone until late and expected us to do what we were supposed to and not fight.

We promised and ate our supper quietly. We didn't dare speak of the possibility of Mutti coming back.

That night, we went to bed without our parents. When I woke up the next morning, something was different. I sneaked out of the bedroom, and when I looked at the sofa bed, I expected Vati to lie there asleep, as he had done for the last several weeks. My heart skipped a beat. A sudden anger, mixed with delight and elation, rose in my breast. Lying next to him, as if she'd never been gone, was my Mutti. I told myself not to be angry. She was gone and now was back. Nothing else mattered. Mutti had returned. Things would go back to normal. If we'd just pretend they would, we'd all be happy again.

22

THE BATTLE IS WON, BUT NOT THE WAR

THE LIGHT RAIL ARRIVES, ALMOST EMPTY. WE PICK A SEAT.

"It's not that I didn't miss you," Mutti said. "I thought of you kids all the time I was gone and cried for you every night. But I couldn't come home. You can see that, can't you?"

I glance at Mutti. Small and humble, she sits next to me. The feisty light in her eyes is gone, and she stares at her wrinkled hands in her lap.

Even so, a bit of the old hurt and anger rises in my heart. "At that time, all I knew was that we missed you and needed you, and you weren't there. You were with Sergey or your sister instead of with us."

"I stayed with Brigitte for a few days. But she was hard to live with. When I left her, I went to Wiesbaden, and the manager of the Traveler's Rest hired me. I worked there for a few weeks." She turns to me. "Believe me, it wasn't fun, and it wasn't easy."

"Then why didn't you come back?"

"I wanted to come back, but it had to be on my terms, not on your father's. Otherwise, he would have never let me live it down. Your father finally came after me and begged me to come back, so I did."

"Maybe you're right," I say. "What about Sergey?"

"He was married. Anyway, he died a long time ago. Look, here's our stop. Let's go home and see what we can whip up for supper."

Mutti gladly changes the subject, but my mind is still on what happened so long ago.

Life did not go back to normal after she returned. Maybe it would have been even worse if Vati hadn't gone and begged her to come back. I can see that now. But I couldn't then.

SUMMER 1959

Mutti was back. Nobody mentioned her leaving, not even Vati. The subject was verboten. Somehow, deep in my heart, I realized something irretrievably bad would happen if anyone mentioned it. Maybe she'd leave again, this time forever. Not talking about it didn't make things any better, but in a way it kept the family functioning.

* * *

"*Pilzchen, essen kommen*!" Mutti's familiar call for Vati rang through the air from the caravan.

I set out seven plates and the flatware. Vati clumped up the caravan stairs and came inside. The sound of his steps made me cringe. It sounded harsh and tight, different from the way he used to enter our caravan.

As Vati came in, Wally slipped into the kitchen from between his legs, and Vati almost stumbled. His face set into hard lines, and his mouth tightened. "Dang beast," he muttered and kicked at Wally. His boot connected with her side with a thump. Wally yelped, pulled in her tail, and fled into the living room behind the cold stove.

My heart thudded in my chest. Vati had always been nice to Wally. He used to talk to her and stroke her between the ears when she lay down on the sofa next to him, even when he was mad at us. Why did he kick her now for no reason?

I wanted to tell him not to do that. I wanted to defend our dog, but when I saw the hard, cold look in his eyes, I shut my mouth and looked at my brother and sisters, who had streamed in after Vati and found their seats. They all stared at Vati. Silence permeated the kitchen.

"What did you that for?" Mutti said. "The poor creature didn't do you any harm. Leave her alone."

"You're the one to speak. Get me my supper and leave me alone. I have work to do."

Mutti pressed her lips together. She piled three potato pancakes onto Vati's plate and set a *Bulette* [fried hamburger meat] next to it.

We ate in silence. Vati wolfed down his food. "I want some coffee," he said.

"I haven't made any yet," Mutti said. "I'll bring you some in a minute."

Vati rose. "What kind of nonsense is that?" he roared. "Am I always last in this home? I've about had it."

He balled his fist and swiped at his plate. It clattered to the linoleum floor but didn't break. Vati stepped around it and left the caravan.

I stared after him with wide eyes, glad he was gone. Mutti picked up the plate and sat back down to finish her meal.

I chewed my last bites. Nothing was the same as it had been before Mutti left. I didn't understand why Vati was mad now so much of the time.

Wasn't he glad she was back? Then I remembered that I too felt angry when she first returned. Maybe Vati was still upset because she had gone. But that was all over, and he should be happy because she was here now.

But Vati didn't laugh and take things as easily as he used to. He was harsh and impatient with us children, more so than ever before.

The easy banter between Vati and Mutti, which used to make me feel safe and loved, was gone. Before, when he teased her, a smile used to make his eyes shine, but now his face was tight and his voice bitter. The slightest provocation made him upset. More than once, when Mutti brought him coffee that was too cold or said something, he stormed from our home, fuming.

He never hit Mutti, but the streaks on the wall where he threw his coffee cup were a mute reminder of their fights for a long time.

That night, and many nights after, I went to sleep with my pillow over my ears, trying to shut out Mutti and Vati's yelling at each other.

"Who do you think you are, a queen?" Vati's voice roared through the thin bedroom wall. "Be glad I took you back."

"You act like an animal, not a human being. Why should I be glad to be back when you treat me like this?"

A crash announced another dish had hit the wall.

I wanted to crawl into a hole somewhere. I pressed my pillow tighter to my ears, screwed my eyes shut, and tried to think of Jesus. Eventually my body relaxed and sweet sleep took over.

When the fighting was too bad, I sometimes thought about running away. But who'd take in a dumb little carnival kid? Also, every time I considered running away, I remembered little Eva. I would miss her. And maybe she would be even lonelier without me.

So I stayed, and the summer wound to an end. Maybe things would be better in winter quarters.

23
WETZLAR

I SNAP TWO PHOTOS OF MUTTI IN FRONT OF THE TABERNACLE ON Temple Square and ask a woman passing by to take a picture of us together.

We wander off. Mutti looks back. "What a nice place Salt Lake City is. It's almost as large as Berlin was when I was young. Not like that tiny Wetzlar, where we ended up."

"I've always loved Wetzlar," I say.

"I guess it was better than those country places where we ran the carnival during the summer.," Mutti turns to a large display window and admires the new fashions.

Mutti grew up in the greatest city of Europe and can't understand anyone who prefers small-town life. I am her daughter, but I have my own preferences, and despite all our differences, we are forever bound together.

While Mutti chats about Berlin, I remember the city I still call my hometown.

FALL AND WINTER 1959

I sat on the kitchen bench, hugging Wally and looking out the window at the trees passing by in the drizzling rain. The fields of stubble where the wheat had grown in the summer couldn't quite hide behind the bare chestnut trees planted along the road. Fallen leaves littered the shoulder of the street.

Soon we'd be in winter quarters in the same city where we stayed last winter. I would go to the same school again. I stroked Wally and tried to remember the kids. Most of them didn't like me, probably because I was a "carnie," but maybe also because I was so clumsy. Last year, the team leaders always chose me last for any sports we played in PE.

At least we were back in Wetzlar, my hometown. That sounded good. I repeated "my hometown" under my breath so my siblings in the living room wouldn't hear. Wally looked up and pricked her ears, and I smiled and stroked her.

The winter before, Vati decided we needed an address and a place to call our hometown. He chose Wetzlar, a small city in the heart of Hessen, the center of Germany, and rented a post office box there so our mail wouldn't have to follow us around the carnival circuit every summer.

I wanted to stay here forever. One day, I would live in a real house here in Wetzlar. I thought of the little garden gnomes that graced the front lawns of so many of the homes I had admired during the summers. I would have a big, roomy house and a garden gnome. And flowers in my front yard.

Now the road widened, houses flanking the sides. A yellow sign welcomed us to the home of the Leitz Company, which made Leica cameras. One of the Leica cameras had traveled all the way into space. I peered past the cars whizzing by and at the businesses that, bit by bit, replaced smaller family houses. A bakery, followed by a butcher shop, greeted us.

Vati stopped at a traffic light. How bright the red and green colors shone when we first stopped, then passed. The little towns where we held our carnival in the summers never had traffic lights.

Our caravan didn't drive through the old part of the city. Instead, we tuck-tucked past large buildings with tiny windows. One of these had to be the Leitz factory.

We followed the train tracks for a while and then turned left into a narrow lane not too far from the tracks. The sound of a train whistle accompanied us as we turned into our winter quarters, a large empty space by the sawmill, the same place I remembered from last year.

But it wasn't empty now. I stared out the window, forgetting I was petting Wally.

Another caravan with a pack trailer behind it, this one painted gray, not glossy brown like our own, stood along the fence that separated our place from the lumberyard.

A boy of about thirteen, hugging a large German shepherd, sat on the caravan's stairs. Four dark brown, inquisitive eyes, the dog's and the boy's, watched our incoming caravan. The dog, happy to see something happening, wagged its tail, and the boy stroked him between the ears. I already liked that boy; he had a dog too.

Vati positioned our caravan next to the other one and connected the stairs to the front. We children couldn't wait to leave our home and check out the other family. We had neighbors for the first time in my life.

Mutti checked the cabinets to make sure nothing had broken during the trip and finally allowed us to go out and inspect the new neighbors. Wally bounded down the stairs and rushed between Vati's legs, eager to make friends with the new dog.

Vati said a harsh word in Polish and kicked at Wally. My heart constricted as Wally yelped and slunk away. Vati muttered under his breath and turned to the back of the caravan to connect the electricity. I let out my breath, relieved he didn't yell at us or start another fight with Mutti.

I followed Franz and Josefa down the steps. Together we neared the other caravan, where a teenage girl had joined the boy.

Carmen approached the girl, who was about two years older than she was. Carmen introduced herself, and the girl answered. She spoke with a strong Polish accent. Her name was Antje, and her brother was called Hubert.

Hubert smiled and petted his dog, who, tail wagging, sniffed Wally's behind.

"Where are you from?" I asked Antje.

"Poland. But we live here now."

"I'm in my last year of school. Do you still go?" Carmen asked.

"No, I'm already sixteen, but Hubert has to go."

Carmen smiled and came closer. Soon the two girls were talking with their backs to us smaller girls.

I glanced at Hubert.

"Where do you go to school?" Franz asked him.

"Iding Schule, but I only have to go until December. Then I'll start an apprenticeship."

I wished I could quit school too. Hubert seemed very adult to me.

I pushed between the two boys. "I have to go two more years. How come you all live in a caravan too if you don't travel?"

"We had a carnival in Poland. But here in Germany, we don't want to travel. We'll get an apartment in Neustadt, as soon as one becomes available, probably next summer. My Vati already works at Buderus, and Antje works in a store downtown."

I sighed. "I wish we could live in an apartment too. It would be great not to travel all the time."

Hubert waved his hand. "I don't really care. But I like it here in Germany. Things are so different than they are in Poland."

Hubert turned to my brother. "Do you guys want to play? It's really fun in the sawmill. We can play hide-and-seek there in the evenings when the workers are gone."

The door to his caravan opened and a plain, gray-haired woman called him and Antje to come in.

Hubert waved at her, his eyes on Franz. "Come on out after supper, and we'll play." He turned and ran up the steps into his home.

* * *

We spent many winter nights playing hide-and-seek and other games among the stacks of planks and boards in the sawmill. Carmen considered herself too grown up to join our play. She and Antje sat on the stairs or went for walks together when the weather was good, and when it wasn't, they spent their time in one or the other caravan.

That winter, instead of fixing up the old merry-go-round and repainting the pictures, Vati drew up plans and built a new attraction modeled after the Hula-Hoop. A partner put up the money, and Vati bought the steel and the wood, took out his old acetylene torch, and, on the open space in front of our caravan, welded large steel beams together.

The new attraction turned out to be a merry-go-round with steel wheels running on top of a metal circle held up by wooden and metal beams. The whole thing looked like a large drum with wheels all around it. Each of the circles held two swinging seats, a lot like the seats on a Ferris wheel.

* * *

As winter wore on, things settled down between my parents. The fighting diminished and eventually disappeared. Vati smiled and joked with Mutti and us again. In the evenings, Mutti and Vati played chess or read books, companionably sitting next to each other on the sofa.

I watched them as I got ready for bed, listened to their banter through the closed bedroom door, and thanked God in my quiet prayers that Mutti and Vati were happy again. In spite of the cold, the snow, and the constantly overcast sky, light and happiness accompanied me, and I reveled in our newfound peace. Things were going to be all right.

That New Year's we had a small party with our neighbors. Vati and Mutti and the neighbor couple sat on the sofa, drinking and talking in Polish.

We older children amused ourselves with a new and fun way of telling the future. Mutti had bought a kit that contained six tiny lead figures, a steel spoon, a tin cup, and a candle. While we waited for midnight, we children, with Antje and Hubert, crowded around the kitchen table, where we lit the candle. Each of us melted a piece of lead on a steel spoon over the candle and dropped it into the cup, which we had filled with water, according to the instructions. When the lead cooled and hardened, we took it out of the water and inspected the new form, trying to read a hint of what might happen in the next year.

My little form came out. I inspected it. It had the shape of a baby.

"Look! We're going to have a new baby," I called.

Mutti, in the living room, stopped in midsentence. She stared at me, a frown on her face. I didn't understand why she was mad. Had I done something wrong? Maybe I shouldn't have yelled.

"What a silly idea. You always talk such nonsense." She turned back to Antje's mother.

24

ANOTHER ARGUMENT

I<small>T'S EVENING. KEN AND MY DAUGHTERS ARE WATCHING THEIR</small> favorite TV show in the living room. Their laughter drifts into the kitchen, where Mutti and I are going through another pile of old photos she brought with her.

I hold out one of them. "Look at this, Mutti." In the black-and-white picture, our whole family is depicted, sitting on the steps of Vati's new attraction, little Eva nestled between me and fifteen-year-old Carmen. "I remember when it was taken. That was on the first warm day of the year, in March 1960."

Mutti picks up the photo. "I remember too. Your Vati was almost done building the Hula-Hoop attraction."

"Hula-Hoops were so in fashion that year. Look, even Wally is in that photo. We all look so happy."

"Things were better that winter," Mutti says. "But I paid for that."

Mutti puts down the photo and turns to another one, an earlier snapshot of us children.

Mutti's remark brings back the argument I had

VATI'S NEW ATTRACTION

overheard not long before the photo with the Hula-Hoop was taken.

MARCH 1960

Class let out early because my last-hour teacher in sixth grade was ill. Alone, I marched along the narrow cobblestone streets of downtown Wetzlar toward the sawmill. I wandered past the old houses that surrounded the town well and admired their white stucco façades framed in dark brown beams. At the well, I stopped and ran my hand through the water that splashed from the cast-iron pipes into the large metal tub.

Cars lumbered by on the narrow one-way street. Here the streets were only one-way because they were so old and narrow. But at the corner, a traffic light separated the old road from a newer asphalt one. I took this road to get to the industrial district and our winter quarters.

I stopped in front of a bakery, deeply inhaling the fragrance of the fresh goodies drifting from the entrance. Shiny, dark loaves of rye bread gleamed in the window, and a torte covered in whipped cream and cherries invited shoppers to enter.

The sun's heat made me take off my coat, and I carried it over my arm. With the warm sunshine on my back, I walked on. I neared our caravan, whose door stood open. The neighbor's door was closed. Antje was at work, and Hubert was still in school with my brother and sisters. Their mother must have gone shopping.

The sun highlighted the first shy green on the birches between the sawmill and our caravan. It warmed the ground. Small daisies had sprung up to the side of our home. I bent to look them over. Maybe I'd pick some and put them into a water glass for the kitchen table.

From our caravan, Mutti's loud voice rang out with a harsh edge. "I can't believe this happened again," she said. "I'm almost forty!"

"Maybe you should see someone," Vati ventured.

"That's dangerous." Mutti's voice wavered. "Besides, it's the end of the winter, and we don't have that kind of money. Later it will be too late."

A pause.

"Don't cry," Vati said. "It's not the end of the world."

"What do you know?" She sobbed. "I can't believe you'd do that to me again."

It didn't sound at all like the fights Mutti and Vati had after she came back home. This time it was Mutti who was angry with Vati. What were they arguing about?

I stared at the flowers in my hand. Maybe they would make her happy, but she'd be mad if I came into the caravan now. She didn't like it if we saw her crying.

I dropped the flowers onto the grass and turned away, ashamed for listening and vaguely sorry because of Mutti's crying. I trudged to the uncultivated field on the other side of the sawmill and played among the dead tree stumps that littered the edge of the field. The weather over time had gnawed a deep indentation into the side of one of the stumps. It looked like a little throne, just right for a girl my age. I sat on it and pretended I was a queen. Wally, who had followed me, was my minister. I, as the queen, granted all children the right to live in real houses. The queen, however, didn't need a house, because she lived in the castle. I looked the other tree stumps over and made them each into different rooms of my castle. I found a place just right for a bed between two of the stumps. I was getting ready to lie in my queenly, grass-covered bed when I heard Hubert call to my brother—the other children were home.

By the time I joined them, ready to go in and have some supper, I had forgotten about the argument I'd overheard.

25

MICHAEL

I GIVE MY YOUNGEST DAUGHTER TWENTY DOLLARS AND HUG HER good-bye. She's going to the beach with her boyfriend's family.

After Meagan leaves, Mutti turns to me. "You had it much easier with your six children. It was so hard with all you kids in a caravan. Sometimes I didn't know what to do first. And then Michael came."

"I thought that was so exciting," I say. "But I was just a kid, only twelve."

"It might have been exciting for you. For me, it was extra work piled on top of all the work I already had."

I was a bit older that year, and I remember the stress and pain Mutti suffered. She seldom smiled that summer and was sick a lot. I pat her back. "We did all right, in spite of everything."

"Easy for you to say," Mutti grumbles, her face set with memories of her own.

SUMMER 1960

That summer, Mutti grew heavier. She was short-tempered and often sick. Many times Carmen and I ran the shooting gallery on our own while Mutti stayed at home reading one of her beloved doctor novels.

One day, Carmen and I were running the shooting gallery. The fairgrounds lay deserted. It was too late for the afternoon kids and too early for the evening crowd. I picked up a red paper rose to stick into one of the little pipes customers were supposed to hit so the flower would fall.

Carmen came up to me. "Do you know Mutti is P-R-E-G-N-A-N-T?" she whispered.

"She's what?"

"Pregnant, dummy. We're going to have a new baby," Carmen said.

I stopped, the red rose in my hand. I had wondered why Mutti was getting so big. Now I knew. A new baby. My prophecy from New Year's Eve was really coming true.

"I knew that," I lied. "I knew it all along. Remember, my piece of lead on New Year's came out looking like a baby."

Carmen sneered. "Pure coincidence," she said and stalked off.

I replaced the flower and leaned against the counter, smiling. I couldn't wait to have a new baby to hug and take for walks in a baby buggy. Maybe people would think I was the mother. That would make me feel so grown up!

One day, about two weeks into August, I was washing the lunch dishes. Josefa dried them and put them away. I thought about the upcoming fall festival in my hometown.

"Soon we'll be back in Wetzlar," I said. "Maybe we'll see Antje and her family."

But Josefa didn't respond. She held a plate in one hand and a drying towel in the other and stared into the living room.

Silence permeated the caravan. The warm summer rain made a soft, musical patter on the windowpane. I wondered why Franz and Eva, in the living room with Mutti, were so quiet. I dropped the washcloth and turned to look.

The first thing I saw was seven-year-old Eva. She sat on the sofa, quiet as a mouse and sucking her thumb! She hadn't done that for a long time. I was just about to open my mouth and shame her, when I noticed what Mutti was doing.

Her old suitcase sat on the living room table, wide open. So was the drawer over the bedroom door, where she stashed her clothes. Mutti, her face drawn, held two bras in her hands and transferred them to the suitcase.

My heart plummeted into my shoes. I couldn't catch my breath. Was she leaving us again, this time for good? I opened my mouth, but not a sound escaped. I was afraid to say anything for fear that whatever I said would be the thing that would make her leave for good. I envied Eva's thumb-sucking. I wished I had something warm and comforting to cling to.

"Where are you going?" Josefa, next to me, said in a small voice.

Mutti looked up and frowned.

"Are you coming back?" I asked.

Mutti's dark eyes focused on me. Before she could answer, I heard heavy steps on the stairs outside. The door opened, and Vati entered.

He pushed Josefa and me to the side and turned to Mutti. "Are you ready?"

Mutti frowned at him. "Not yet. I still need to pack the things for the baby."

A long sigh escaped my lips.

Mutti turned and stared at me. "Vati is taking me to Wetzlar to have the baby."

Eva pulled the thumb from her mouth and hid it in her dress pocket. "When are you coming back?"

"I'll see you when you all get to Wetzlar. Just be good and mind your father, okay?"

We all nodded. Franz ran to Vati. "Can I go with you?"

Vati dropped onto the sofa, watching Mutti pack. "No, there won't be much room in the car. And I need a man to watch over the women while I'm gone."

Josefa sat on the arm of the sofa, near Vati. "Mutti, can't you stay a while longer? Until we get to Wetzlar?"

Mutti explained that the baby would be coming any time now, and she didn't want to wait around to have it in the middle of nowhere. She packed a white sweater into the suitcase, turned back to the drawer, and brought out the tiny baby clothes in blue, pink, and light green.

She finished packing while we chattered about the new baby. We wondered if the baby would be another girl, or maybe a boy, as Franz hoped.

Mutti closed the suitcase and stretched her back. "You kids, don't fight, and make sure to help each other. And I want a clean home when I return, hear?"

We assured her we would be like the angels in heaven. Vati took the suitcase and opened the door. Mutti waddled down the steps after him, and my sisters, brother, and I followed. Vati helped Mutti into the VW and started it. As he eased from the fairgrounds, we waved until the car went around a corner and we couldn't see it anymore.

* * *

Michael was born on August 30, ten days after Mutti turned forty. She stayed in the hospital until the second week of September, when we traveled to Wetzlar to be part of their fall festival. Once he established us on the fairgrounds, Vati took the VW to get Mutti and the new baby from the hospital.

We were all waiting in front of the caravan when he returned. He opened the door for Mutti, and she emerged from the car. She held a light blue bundle to her heart. Mutti looked rested and healthy. Her black eyes shone, and her hair glinted in the sunlight. She smiled.

We crowded around her, but she waved us off. "Let me get in first," she said. "You can look at your new brother later."

Inside, she placed Michael into his baby buggy, where he would sleep for the next several months. We children crowded around and admired the sleeping baby, with his tiny fists curled next to his fat cheeks.

26
A DEATH

MUTTI AND I SIT AT THE KITCHEN TABLE IN MY SPACIOUS HOME IN Provo, a bouquet of roses in front of us. The bright August sun streams through the glass patio doors into the kitchen, painting the roses a bright bloodred.

"I never thought I'd live that long," Mutti says. "When I was young, and trying to find a way out of Berlin, I used to think if I only could make it to the year 2000, that would be so great. And now here it is, way past 2000, and I'm still alive."

"You won't die for a long time yet, Mutti," I say. "You're so strong and healthy."

"I'm not planning to die either. But when my time comes, I hope you'll come to Germany to see me off."

The sweet fragrance of the roses permeates the air, causing a sudden sadness to wash over me. I remember another time when I smelled roses and death.

SEPTEMBER 1960

I sat at my usual kitchen seat, staring out the window at a field riotous with cultivated red and yellow roses in full bloom. A flimsy, short, wire fence separated them from the fairgrounds. The wind rushed over the petals, and, here and there, a few floated to the ground, like tiny red and yellow boats on a calm sea.

As soon as Vati had settled the caravan and connected the steps, I flew outside, Wally at my heels. I ran to the fence and, with my face against the wire, took deep breaths of the lovely fragrance. Wally bounded around me, sniffing out the new smells of this place and wagging her tail. We were in Rosenheim, our last venue for that summer, to provide the entertainment for the city's annual rose festival.

The next morning on my way to school, I still smelled the roses. I couldn't wait to see the rose parade that Saturday.

When I came home from the second day of school, Mutti sat on the sofa. She rocked Michael in the baby buggy with one hand and held the book she was reading with the other. Every time she quit rocking, little Michael fussed.

Wally ran up to me, but her tail wasn't wagging, and she whined. I tried to pet her, but she turned and ran back to her box by the stove. Maybe she didn't like all these roses. Their smell surely must have messed up her nose.

"What's the matter with Wally?" I asked.

"Oh, good. You're here. Come and rock the baby," Mutti said. "I need to get Wally's box ready."

I slipped my satchel from my shoulders, pushed it under the coffee table with my foot, and asked, "Ready for what?"

"She is about to have her puppies."

"Oh."

During the summer, Wally too had been getting heavier. Soon we realized that she had managed to get herself pregnant, in spite of the care Mutti always took to keep her away from other dogs when she was in heat.

"I haven't watched her like I should have." Mutti shook her head and moved the box further behind the stove. "I thought she was too old for this. And now she'll have puppies. Just what we need with the new baby and all."

I was hardly listening. The puppies were on the way! I couldn't wait to tell Josefa. While rocking the buggy, I craned my neck. Mutti moved the chair from the coffee table to the corner by the stove, in front of Wally's box. She sat on it, and Wally waddled under the chair legs and settled into her box. Mutti obstructed the view, and I couldn't see what was happening.

Eva came in from school and shrugged off her satchel. Mutti shushed her. Experimentally, I stopped rocking. No sound came from the buggy. I checked. "He's asleep, Mutti."

Mutti whispered back to move him into the bedroom.

I pushed the baby buggy into the back room and closed the door. Then I squeezed into the corner by the stove, trying to see what went on in Wally's box. But Mutti told me to go into the kitchen and keep Eva busy so that Wally could have her babies in peace.

Vati came in and lit another cigarette. Enveloped by the reassuring smell of Vati's smoke, Eva and I played old maid at the kitchen table.

When Josefa came home, she stared at Vati and Mutti, who were bent over Wally's box.

"Wally is having her babies," I said.

"It's moving," Mutti said. "Look! I think this one is fine."

A little later Vati shook his head. "This one isn't." He scooped something out of the box.

"Can we see?" I asked as he strode through the kitchen, his hands cupped around a still, dark form.

Eva rose and craned her neck to see what Vati held in his hands.

"This one is dead," Vati said as he went by us and opened the door to outside. "You can see the live ones later."

He returned, his hands empty.

Finally, for the fifth time, Vati straightened from the box with a little shape in his hands. He declared in a low, sad voice, "This one is dead too."

My eyes smarted. Poor Wally. She was losing all her children. I hoped they would all go to heaven. Then she would see them again one day.

"How many are alive?" Carmen, from the corner of the kitchen door, wanted to know.

"Four are okay," Vati said. "I think she's done now. You girls, get to bed. You can see them tomorrow."

I breathed a sigh of relief. Wally wouldn't feel too bad about losing some if she still had four babies to feed and take care of.

I took my turn at the washbowl, and as I wiped my face, I saw movement from the corner of my eye.

Wally pulled herself to her feet with a small yelp. She stood over her four tiny pups and gave each a lick. Then she turned and looked at Vati, Mutti, and me. With a low whine she limped to the door and waited for Vati to open it.

"She probably has to go to the bathroom," Carmen said.

I stared at a bright red drop of blood on the kitchen linoleum. She better come back soon. She needed to rest.

I lay in bed listening for Wally's whine to be let back in, but before I heard it, I fell asleep.

The next morning when I got up, Mutti sat among the pillows of the sofa bed, feeding baby Michael. Michael made little slurping noises while he nursed and pressed a small fist against her nightgown.

I glanced at her and hurried to the dog box. There, nestled in the old rags, lay four tiny whimpering bundles, and no Wally. I turned to Mutti, who looked at me, frowning. "Where's Wally?" I asked.

I heard Carmen rummaging in the kitchen. She called, "She hasn't come home. I'm looking for that doll bottle you had, to feed the puppies with."

I went into the kitchen. "Why don't we wait for Wally to feed them?"

"I don't know if Wally will come home," Mutti called from the sofa bed. "The birth was hard on her. And if she isn't home by now . . ." Her voice trailed off. Her eyes looked sad.

I opened my mouth to protest but closed it again. I stared at the puppies without seeing them. Wally would surely come home. She'd never run away from her children. We just needed to wait a little longer. *She will come home, she will come home*, I repeated over and over in my mind.

But what if she didn't? I remembered the blood from last night, and sudden tears tingled my eyes. I blinked furiously to keep the tears at bay. Wally couldn't be dead, she just couldn't. I pushed this unbearable thought from my mind and went into the kitchen to help Carmen find the bottle. We rummaged in the toy drawer, all the while hoping for a scratching on the door, for an impatient whimpering. It never came. Mutti put the drowsy Michael back into the baby buggy, pulled on her dress, and came into the kitchen. She searched the food drawer and pulled out a can of milk.

Vati came in, holding the empty refuse bucket.

"Can you make the bed?" Mutti asked him. "I need to feed the pups."

Vati didn't even grumble. He pushed the bucket behind the curtain. In the living room, he folded the blankets, clicked the sofa back into place, and stashed the blankets underneath.

Mutti warmed a little milk and water in a small pot on the gas stove. "Go on out, all of you, and see if you can find Wally."

Franz followed Carmen, Josefa, and me into the foggy morning. Together we looked under the rosebushes and in the tall weeds.

"Wally!" I called, searching the bushes for a sign of movement. "Here, girl! Come home, Wally!" I used my loudest voice, but to no avail.

The smell of the roses invaded my nostrils. It wasn't sweet at all now. It made my empty stomach clench. I wished the roses wouldn't look so cheerful. Nothing was cheerful to me that morning.

I pushed the rosebushes aside with a stick, but I was afraid to look too closely. I didn't want to find a dead Wally, a damp, furry dog body with empty eyes and stiff legs stretched out. We wandered around, calling with all our might, hoping she was just lost, would hear us, and would follow our voices home.

When Eva complained that her stomach hurt, we gave up calling and trudged back home. Mutti had some buns and hot cocoa for us, and we ate in a silence punctuated by tiny whimpers from the stove corner.

The remaining two days in Rosenheim, when we children weren't rocking the baby, washing dishes, or helping with the carnival, we searched every inch of the surrounding fields we could get to. We didn't forget the trees and gardens on the other side, either. I walked around town for what seemed like hours, checking bushes and the trees in the orchards. No one could find Wally.

Sure she had died, we finally gave up. When we pulled up stakes and left, I sat in my corner by the kitchen window, Eva next to me and Carmen and Josefa crowding in front of me. All of us stared out the window in one last effort to find Wally. But no small, black-and-white furball burst from the roses or the surrounding bushes to hurl herself into the caravan at the last moment, as she had done so often before.

We were left with four tiny pups.

Mutti, busy with the new baby, told Carmen and me how to feed the pups. We tried to keep them alive with the doll bottle, but within days they too died. Through my tears and sadness, I told myself that now Wally was in heaven with all her children and was happy.

But I wasn't. I wandered around for weeks, missing her. While we traveled back to Wetzlar for winter quarters, I kept touching the kitchen seat next to me. But my hand didn't find a warm, furry body, and my ears waited in vain for the snuffle and whine so typical of Wally. Wally, my best friend, the one who never judged me and always accepted me, was dead. I guess a girl grows up when her beloved friend and confidante dies. I grew up that winter.

27

LEARNING

W E ARE AT THE OFFICE SUPPLY STORE, CHECKING OUT THE BACK-to-school specials. A colorful display of notebooks and other supplies draws my attention.

"Liesel and Meagan will need binders and paper." I pick four binders in different colors and put them into my shopping cart. "I ought to get them some more pencils too."

"The amount of time grown children spend in school these days," Mutti grumbles. "I didn't have a chance to go to school through my teen-age years. At that time, we graduated from elementary school at fourteen and went right into an apprenticeship."

"I had only eight years of school too. Remember?"

"There was no way for you to get more education so soon after the war. We couldn't afford private schools, and you needed to help in the carnival."

I hear the defensiveness in her voice, and I understand that times were different then. And everything turned out all right for me after all.

I didn't go back to school until I was a young mother in America, but I still remember how much I learned when I was thirteen, even though I didn't learn it in school.

WINTER 1960–61

I sat in the corner on the kitchen bench and stared out the window at the sawmill. Icy rain shrouded the open-sided shed where clumps of boards and logs lay huddled like tired ghosts in a monstrous coffin.

I wished I had something to do. Maybe I should go out to play despite the cold.

Eva yelled from the living room, "Stop it, Franz! Stop it!"

Franz backed into the kitchen, holding a blue stuffed dog and laughing. He moved one more step and accidentally kicked baby Michael, who lay on a blanket on the kitchen floor. The baby joined Eva in her screams. Josefa, on the other side of the kitchen table, slapped her math book shut and pressed the heels of her hands to her ears.

"Quit that noise, Eva!" Mutti yelled into the confusion. She rushed from the living room, where she had sat on the sofa, reading, scooped up the sobbing baby, and sent Franz outside to help Vati. That winter, Vati was building a new attraction for us older girls to run in the summer.

Carmen squeezed past Mutti, went to the hook by the door where our coats piled high on top of each other, and pulled hers out from under mine. "I'm going to the youth center."

"Go on, go on. One less child to make noise." Mutti marched to the bedroom, where she placed the still wailing Michael onto one of the beds and closed the door.

I came from my corner. "Can I go with her?"

I had never been to the youth center. Antje, who now lived in an apartment, had told Carmen about it. Carmen, who was already finished with school, had gone several times. I wanted to be a youth like her, not a kid. After all, I was almost done with school too.

"Take her with you, Carmen," Mutti said.

Carmen grumbled under her breath, opened the door, and hurried out.

I grabbed my coat and ran after my sister. My breath formed rime on my upturned coat collar, and I stuffed my already cold hands deep into my pockets.

On the narrow cobblestone streets, I rushed to keep up with Carmen. We walked past the city center and up the hill. And there I saw it. Bordering the marketplace near the cathedral, an ordinary house with a sign in front squeezed between a bakery and the city hall.

We stepped in, and warmth caressed my icy face. I found myself in a hallway with a check-in counter to the side. A smiling young woman in a white sweater asked us to sign our names and ages in a large book.

She read my name and looked up. "Is this your first time here? You're a bit young."

Sure she would send me home again, I nodded. I glanced up the dark hallway. Voices drifted through the doors. Maybe being sent home wasn't so bad. After all, I was pretty young. Maybe everybody would make fun of me.

"I see you're thirteen. You're old enough," the young woman said with a smile. "Check out our center. We have a game room, a reading room, and a place where you can visit and talk. Enjoy yourself."

I followed Carmen. A large green table with many different-colored and numbered balls on it dominated the room. Girls and boys bustled around with long sticks. They bumped the balls, laughed, and talked.

"That's pool," Carmen said. "It's a fun game. Maybe they'll let you play when you're older."

Smaller tables and chairs crowded the walls. Young people milled around. Laughter and calls flew through the air. In a corner, a group of four played Aggravation amid outbursts of frustration and encouragement.

Carmen left, and I watched for a while, but nobody invited me to play. They didn't seem to notice me. I went after Carmen to the next room. There, a fire crackled in a fireplace. It was warm, and the dancing flames fascinated me. I went closer and stared at them until my surroundings distracted me. Fuzzy brown and green easy chairs surrounded the tables in this room. The chairs, though worn, looked comfortable enough to fall asleep in them.

The kids here were Carmen's age or older. I stood by the fire, warming my back. Carmen talked with a group of three boys and two girls. A skinny boy with glasses glanced at me but didn't say anything.

I wondered if I should join them. But they were a lot older than I was, at least sixteen, and surely they wouldn't want me there. I left my sister talking to the boy and his friends and went to explore the next room.

A shelf crowded with books of many sizes and colors covered one complete wall. On both sides of the door, racks of magazines displayed their colorful covers. A few kids sat at tables, leafing through books and magazines. A boy about my age leaned back on a sofa with closed eyes, an open book on his lap.

The magazines, with their red and green covers, drew me in. It seemed I was free to look at any of them without having to ask or to pay. I pulled out a bound set of *Pfadfinder* [Boy Scout magazines], sat on the sofa at the opposite end of the sleeping boy, and read an article about the Wright

Brothers, who had invented the airplane in America. How interesting! I leafed through other magazines, reading about strange frogs in South America, how to build a kite, and many other fascinating things.

I don't know how long I stayed there enjoying the sudden discovery of a world I hadn't realized existed. The boy on the other side of the sofa woke, rubbed his eyes, and gave me a sheepish glance. Shortly after he left, Carmen came.

"There you are," she said. "I've been looking all over for you. We need to get home. Come on."

I rose, shelved my magazines, and followed her back to our world of noise and disharmony.

* * *

As the weeks passed, I went to the youth center whenever I could. Mutti was glad to have me out of the house, and soon I found my way there by myself. When Carmen was with me, she played pool or board games with the others, listened to music, and joined animated discussions in the other rooms.

For me, the world lay waiting to be discovered in the reading room. I spent hours reading the magazines, and eventually I touched the books. And they, in turn, touched me in ways I never imagined.

Jack London's tales of Alaska and half-wild dogs took me to a place and a way of life so different from mine, but still like mine, because I too had had a dog and loved it. I understood the dogs, who never questioned their masters and did what they asked.

I read *Romeo and Juliet in the Country* by Gottfried Keller, and my heart broke at the fate of the hapless young couple from feuding farming families.

One day, I picked a book at random because it had a strange title, *The Chronicles of Narnia: The Lion, the Witch and the Wardrobe.* I started reading and never stopped. That night, I dreamt of the noble lion. The next day, I walked to the library to check it out so I could read it whenever I wanted. I paid a five-pfennig piece and could keep the book for two weeks, but I finished it in two days. In the analogy with Aslan, the lion, I realized that the writer wrote about Christ, not some lion in an imagined world. The writer tried to tell his readers how wonderfully Christ's sacrifice affects a repentant person. I glowed in the realization that I wasn't the only person who loved God, and I longed to be someplace where I could learn more about my Savior.

I read many other books at the youth center, and eventually I talked to some of the kids. I even learned to play pool, but I was guarded and never made any real friends, except for the books and magazines, which were more than friends to me. After all, the other children might laugh at me, but books didn't judge.

* * *

In March, I went to school for the last time. In a small assembly, the principal praised the eighth grade and handed each of us a certificate of completion of school, which I proudly carried home.

A few weeks later, Vati finished the new attraction we girls would run that summer. We admired the octagonal booth, where customers would throw Ping-Pong balls into different-colored holes on the table in the center. Vati disassembled it and stashed it into the pack trailer. It was time to go.

We six children squeezed into our caravan. With a sigh, Mutti told us to be good and to not destroy anything. Then she took the baby and got into our car, which Vati had connected to the caravan with the tow bar. We were ready to start another carnival circuit.

23

SPACE

MUTTI COMES DOWN THE STAIRS INTO THE LIVING ROOM, CROSSES it, and enters the kitchen. She looks out the glass doors into the sunlit backyard, where irises grow in purple and white profusion along the fence. Two large fir trees overshadow a small patio.

"What space you have here!" she exclaims. "After Michael was born, I felt like I was suffocating in the caravan. You three older girls were getting so big, and then I still had Franz, Eva, and Michael. I didn't know what to do or where to turn."

"I remember. We were awfully crowded. But Vati took care of that, didn't he?"

"Yes, I don't know what I would have done otherwise."

SPRING 1961

We arrived at another town's fairgrounds. Vati settled the caravan, and we girls burst out, ready to inspect the new town. A water pump with its metal trough attracted my attention from across the street. Three boys, probably a bit older than I was, sat on their bikes. They talked and laughed with two girls. One young girl about my age, her light brown hair still in braids, played with the handle of the water pump. A trickle of water splashed into the trough.

They laughed and glanced at us from the corners of their eyes. I wanted to move closer, maybe get in on the conversation, but I was distracted by an unusual sight near our caravan on the fairgrounds.

Another caravan sat on the far side of the fairgrounds. It consisted of three large wagons and one smaller one in a gorgeous brown color. It looked newly painted. Four small, dirty-looking kids played catch in the grass nearby.

I forgot about the town kids and took a few steps closer to the strange caravan. It didn't look familiar. The owner wasn't any of the other carnies we knew. Vati leaned against the strangers' gray tractor in animated conversation with a tall, black-haired man. I was starting to wander toward them when Mutti called my name. I turned and went back.

Mutti glanced at the man, biting her lip, and turned back to me. "Don't go there."

"Who are they?" I asked, staring at the strange caravan and the tall man. He didn't look German.

"Gypsies. They'll be gone in a few days," Mutti said.

"Won't they stay for the carnival?"

"No, they will leave soon."

I stared at Carmen, who shrugged.

Over the next two days, Vati talked to the Gypsies several times. He didn't seem to be afraid of them or disdain them like Mutti did.

Friday morning before I rose, I sat up in my third-tier bunk bed and slid open the *Oberlicht*, the small window slit on the roof of the caravan. The Gypsy caravan was gone; they must have left during the night. But they hadn't taken all of what was theirs with them. All by itself, close to the fence that separated that part of the carnival grounds from the road, stood the small, beautiful caravan. Vati went up the steps and pulled the door wide open.

I jumped out of bed, slipped into yesterday's clothes, and burst through the living room into the kitchen, where Mutti was feeding Michael mush for breakfast. Michael sat on a block Mutti had placed on the kitchen bench. He stretched his arms and tried to grasp the spoon from her.

"What's Vati doing with the Gypsy caravan?" I asked.

The door opened, and Vati stomped in, a big grin on his face. "It's in really good condition. All it needs is a little touch-up and some cleaning." He turned to me. "Since you, Carmen, and Josefa will live there, you three can clean it up."

"That caravan is for us?" My heart beat faster. Delight and awe spread in my soul. We would have our own place and could do whatever we wanted there!

Vati pulled a paper out of his pocket. He unfolded it and spread it on the table, careful to keep it out of Michael's grasp.

"Look at that," he said to Mutti. "He signed it with three *X*s, because he couldn't write."

Mutti laughed. "It's just as valid this way. I can't wait to have the girls move in."

I hardly heard her. I turned to bring my sisters the good news. In the living room, I collided with Carmen, who had woken from the commotion, and Josefa, who trailed after her.

"What's going on?" Carmen asked, rubbing her eyes.

"We have our own new caravan!" I almost yelled.

We didn't even take time to finish breakfast. With our mouths still full, we filed to the door, but Mutti's voice interrupted us. "You're not going there without some water and rags, so you can start cleaning."

For once in our young lives, we didn't protest. Josefa pulled the bowl from under the stove, and Carmen splashed some water into it from the canister. I grabbed the broom and dustpan from the corner by the door. Carmen found the cleanest of the kitchen rags and the scouring powder, and off we went to inspect our new home.

I stopped when I got nearer, broom clutched in my fist, and stared at the window in awe, my mouth open. The window consisted of three panes. In the center pane, someone had painted a bouquet of wildflowers. Red poppies intermingled with sky-blue cornflowers, framed by their bright green stems and leaves. Their blazing colors and unconscious beauty against the gleaming backdrop of the caravan's glossy mahogany-brown paint took my breath away. I was transported into a world where beauty and love reigned, and where a lonely girl could find peace.

"Come on, Sonja!" Josefa's impatient yell pulled me back to the present.

I catapulted up the steps after my sisters. The outside door opened into what I thought was a spacious living room. It smelled dusty, but I forgot all about the smell when I looked around and was greeted by myself! I blinked and realized I was looking into a full-sized mirror fastened to the closet door next to the entrance.

I followed my sisters to the far end of the room, where a door led to another room. Carmen pulled it open, and we surveyed a rather small bedroom, compared to the large one we occupied with Franz and Eva. A two-tiered bunk bed stood against the farthest wall, and a single bed crowded the side wall.

Carmen plopped on the lower one of the bunk beds and said, "That's where I'll sleep. It looks cozy and warm and comfortable."

"Then I'll take the top," I said. "I love the *Oberlicht* [skylight]. And it's warmer higher up."

"I want the top," Josefa protested.

"I'm older. I get it," I said, and Carmen nodded.

Josefa sighed and sat on the smaller, single bed to claim it.

After we bounced on the mattresses and admired the windows, we cleaned our new home.

Later that day, Mutti brought bedsheets and our feather quilts over and supervised us one last time as we put the sheets onto the mattresses and covered them with the feather quilts.

That summer, we reveled in having our own place. When Eva was good, we invited her into our home. We also allowed Franz, our mean brother, to inspect our home, but he scoffed at it and called it a "girls' nest," so we chased him off.

In the evenings, we occasionally sneaked out and scouted around, looking for willing local kids to talk to. With our own home, we felt grown-up and independent.

But as winter arrived, things changed.

29
ENGLISH CLASSES

O N OUR WAY TO A MALL, MUTTI AND I DRIVE THROUGH AN AREA where many stores have Russian names. I remember Mutti talking Russian and Polish when I was small. Sergey was from Russia.

"Do you still remember your Russian?" I ask Mutti.

"I can still say a few things. It's not like English at all. I don't understand English. I always thought Russian would come in handy after the war. If the Russians had conquered Germany, it would have been the dominant language." She sighs. "But I'm glad they didn't. And now practically everybody in Germany speaks English, just like you."

"I'm glad I got to learn English," I say. "It really helped when I immigrated."

"Yes, and now you live in America."

I know Mutti thinks learning another language was all I got out of the English classes I took when I was fourteen. She will never know how much more I learned because I decided to go to those classes.

OCTOBER 1961

Once again, our little caravan tuck-tucked into Wetzlar for winter quarters. This time I sat in the main room of my sisters' and my own caravan and pressed my nose to the window, the red and blue painted flowers painted next to my face.

I stared into the drizzling rain and wrapped my sweater tighter around me.

Vati pulled our caravans past the familiar train station, where the steam of locomotives joined the thin clouds in the humid air. However, we passed by the small street that led to the sawmill and our winter quarters from the last two years. Vati had told us it wasn't available anymore. The city of Wetzlar planned to put part of an Autobahn system in that area. I craned my neck as we drove past but didn't see any construction work.

The caravan chugged past the old Lutheran church and the open area close to it, where we put up our attractions for the Wetzlar spring carnival. Maybe I could go to church there. But these old churches had no heat, and in the winter it would be very cold inside. I didn't know what time the service was, and my family would laugh at me. I discarded that idea and focused on the path Vati took through the inner city.

We passed by the bridge over the river Lahn and pulled into the *Bachweide*, a large empty space near the city center, where the Lahn and the Dill, a smaller river, met.

Vati situated us on the far side of the rivers, close to the path that led to the Esso gas station on the corner of the bridge. There we would fill our water buckets for the rest of the winter.

Vati connected the platform he had built to connect the two homes and slid the familiar four steps into their new slots on the platform. I burst out of our small home, sweater buttoned up to my chin, longing for the warmth of the big caravan.

Vati had put a small wood stove into the corner of the main room in our girl's caravan. But it was difficult to start a fire, and being teenage girls, we were lazy and often let it go out overnight. In the mornings, shivering in our nightgowns, we didn't want to start a new one. It was easier to just barge into the big home, where the fire was already going and breakfast waited.

As winter wore on, it became very cold in our new little caravan, and we spent less and less time there, except to sleep.

This was the first full winter I didn't have to go to school, but since I never made friends easily, I wouldn't miss it. I had no friends and nothing to look forward to. Josefa would soon graduate too. We didn't have much to do but go to the library and the youth center. At home, we were always underfoot in Mutti's caravan, and Mutti still didn't have the space she so craved.

One day, I sat in the kitchen corner of the big caravan, reading a book from the library.

Mutti squeezed by little Michael, who played on the kitchen floor. "Sonja, Josefa, go into your own caravan or go for a walk. It's nice outside."

I closed my book and glanced out the window. The sun shone like a faint orange ball through the thin clouds, and far off I saw some blue sky. I rose. Josefa came from the living room.

Mutti shooed us. "Go on out. Go, go."

It was cold in the small caravan.

Josefa rose from the small sofa. "Let's go for a walk."

Carmen closed her book, unwrapped herself from her featherbed, and grabbed her coat.

We were wandering around the city, admiring the new fashions in the store windows, when we came across an announcement in a bakery window. The heading caught my attention.

"Learn English for Free," it said. And the caption under it said something like, "English classes offered for free by two young men from the United States." At the very bottom, I read the address of a nearby school, a classroom number, and the date and time of the class.

I stopped and read the words again. I wanted to learn, I wanted to know more than what my sparse school education had given me. And learning another language would be nice. Especially English, which was so popular. I never wanted to know Russian, which Mutti spoke fluently, or Polish, Vati's native tongue. English sounded much better to me. After all, it was the "in" thing.

Carmen and Josefa wandered off. "Wait," I called. I fumbled in my purse for a pencil and a slip of paper and scribbled down the address.

Maybe my sisters would go with me. "It's free," I said. "Let's go together and learn English."

Carmen shrugged. "Why not."

Josefa agreed it would be fun.

We wandered home, talking about learning English and impressing the youth in the towns we traveled to every summer.

While talking with my sisters, I realized how tired I was of the constant travel and the lack of education in my life. The never-ending parade of drunken yokels, who considered me easy prey because I lived in the carnival, often made my life unpleasant in the summers.

It was only November. Maybe this winter I would learn something to change my life somehow. With a new spring in my step, I walked through the drizzling rain toward our caravan.

At seven the following Wednesday evening, we sisters showed up in an empty classroom of the elementary school, where these Americans would hold class.

A row of used student desks and chairs faced a wall with an old-fashioned blackboard in its center. A large slide projector stood in one corner.

Two men stood by the blackboard, talking in a foreign language. They were old, at least twenty, compared to my fourteen. One was tall and dark haired, with summer-blue eyes, and the other one was shorter, had red hair and freckles, and wore glasses. I guessed they were the Americans, but I was too shy to talk to them.

The tall man wiped the chalky blackboard with a dusty rag, and the other one dug in a closet and returned to the board with a box of chalk. They saw us and smiled. We found seats in the back of the room and fumbled for our pencils and notebooks.

A young couple drifted in, followed by three teenagers, two older women, and a man. They took seats behind us and whispered to each other. I watched the two Americans talk to each other in their strange language.

The taller, blue-eyed man turned to the class.

"Good evening. We are your English instructors. My name is Mr. Ellis, and this is my partner, Mr. Bishop."

Mr. Ellis rolled his *R*s and sounded as if he was trying to speak and chew gum at the same time. So that's what an American accent sounds like.

Mr. Bishop didn't say anything. He smiled and seemed content to let Mr. Ellis introduce him.

They handed out registration forms. Since we didn't have an address, we girls entered our post office box number. Mr. Bishop collected the registration forms, and class started.

Spellbound, I listened to the lesson. I repeated the strange English sounds with the other students and took notes in the notebook I bought especially for the class.

To the question, "What's your name?" I learned to answer, "My name is Sonja."

Funny how they spell it so different from the way they say it, I thought, and I told myself to remember that the *e* at the end of many words doesn't get spoken in English.

Finally, Mr. Ellis said, "For your *Hausarbeit* [homework], learn all the words we used today and practice the pronunciation."

He glanced at Mr. Bishop, who opened a large, black briefcase and took out a round slide holder. "Before you leave, we would like to invite you to watch a short slideshow about our church," Mr. Ellis went on. "You're free to go, but the slideshow will only take a few minutes."

The young couple rose and left; three teenagers, two older women, and a man stayed. The ladies frowned and leaned back in their chairs, ready to watch. The young people giggled under their breath, but they quieted when Mr. Bishop turned the projector on and the lights off.

What I heard that night changed my life forever.

30

A SPIRITUAL AWAKENING

I t's Sunday. Mutti comes into the kitchen, where I'm making pancakes for brunch.

"How come you're not in church?" she says. "Don't you go to your strange American church anymore?"

"I still go. I already went this morning," I say.

"Oh. I thought you got smarter as you got older."

"Let's not talk about it. I know how you feel about my church, and you know how I feel, and let's leave it at that. I thought we'd take you to the pool this afternoon."

"Sounds like fun. I'm glad I brought my swimsuit with me."

After we eat, I clean up the kitchen, while Mutti gets her swimsuit and towel. With a twinge of sadness, I realize she'll probably never change. She still doesn't approve of the decision I made the winter I was fourteen, a decision that changed my life so drastically.

That first visit to the free English class taught me so much more than just English. How well I still remember the two Americans putting up their equipment and dimming the lights after the English lesson.

OCTOBER 1961

While I leaned back in my seat, ready to learn about a new church, they started the slide projector and turned on a bulky tape player, similar to the one Vati had used the last few years for his carnival music.

The first picture flashed onto the screen. With the slides accompanying him, the narrator, in impeccable German, told the story of a young man who had seen God and Christ in a vision.

Yes, I thought. *I too saw God's hand in a vision.* My heart beat faster, and warmth enveloped me. Christ loved me. Surely He had helped me get here to learn more about him.

Too soon, the slideshow ended. The two Americans packed away the equipment and spoke to other members of the class. I wanted to talk to them about this man Joseph Smith and his vision, but I was with my sisters.

Carmen pulled me by the arm. "Let's go. I don't want to wait around to be converted."

Josefa was already at the door. We left, practicing our newly learned English on each other.

* * *

During the next week, I kept thinking about what I had learned about God, that He still talks to people. This made perfect sense, since God had always been close to me. Why wouldn't he want to reveal himself to certain special people, to let them know about him? I could hardly wait for the second lesson. English was so much fun, and I looked forward to learning more about God and this strange new church our English teachers came from.

The next Wednesday, Carmen had lost interest, and Josefa couldn't go. Surely this was a sign from God. Without my sisters, it would be so much easier for me to talk about religion. Full of expectation, I returned to English class by myself. After the lesson, the two missionaries told the remaining students about a new holy book that Joseph Smith had translated. They called it a second witness to the Bible, or the Book of Mormon, and held it up together with a Bible. As I listened, my thoughts wandered. I'd never held a Bible in my hands, let alone read anything from it. Maybe I should try to get one somewhere. The Book of Mormon would probably be easier to get. The missionaries would surely sell me one.

When their presentation was over, Mr. Ellis and Mr. Bishop cleaned the blackboard and put away the chalk, their Bible, and the Book of Mormon. They shook hands with the students and smiled and talked to them. I hung back and waited for a moment when they weren't busy with someone else.

Finally, Mr. Ellis came up to me. He held a registration card in his hand. "You only gave a post box number. Where do you live?"

"It's hard to explain. We don't really have an address. We live in the Bachweide."

"Where is that?"

My heart beat faster. If they knew where we lived, maybe they would tell me more about their church. On the other hand, my family probably wouldn't like to meet them since they were from a church. I made up my mind. "Why don't you come with me, and I'll show you? It's not very far."

"We could do that. Then we'd know where you all live."

He talked to Mr. Bishop, and soon they were ready to accompany me home.

The two men walked by my side through the quaint inner city with its crooked cobblestone streets and tiny stores. The streetlamps marked faint circles here and there on the narrow sidewalks. Their light highlighted Mr. Ellis's face as he talked to me about what he called the restored gospel.

A half-moon shone through scattered clouds, and a wet wind blew, but I wasn't cold. We walked on, Mr. Ellis by my side, and Mr. Bishop next to him. Mr. Ellis told me about God's love for all mankind, and that's why he restored his true Church upon this earth.

"What did you think about the filmstrip we showed last week?" he asked.

"I would like to hear more about that. I believe in God and that He helps people." I slowed and turned to him. "If God really would restore his Church, he'd do that through a prophet. That makes sense to me."

"Do you think your parents would be interested to hear more?"

I knew they wouldn't, Vati being a non-practicing Catholic, and Mutti, an agnostic Protestant with a Jewish background. But I said yes anyway, because I wanted to hear more, and I was afraid that if I'd tell them my family wasn't interested, they wouldn't talk to me either.

At about nine that evening, we walked past the Esso gas station, down a small path, and entered the Bachweide. Our caravan, lit by the moonlight, was hunkered next to the wire fence, the light shining through the window inviting me back home. My heart was pounding as I ran up the steps and invited the Americans to come in.

"Hi!" I called as I opened the door. Mutti and Vati sat on the sofa in the living room, and Carmen, Franz, and Josefa crowded around the kitchen table, playing cards. The two little ones were already in bed. "These two Americans would like to meet you."

Vati, always agreeable with strangers, led them into the living room and invited them to sit on the sofa. He pulled a kitchen chair into the living room next to the coffee table, sat, and asked about the missionaries' country and families. He even remembered an English word or two from after the war.

During a lull in the conversation, Mr. Ellis leaned forward and focused on my father. "We are missionaries from The Church of Jesus Christ of Latter-day Saints. We want to testify to you that God still speaks to mankind today through his holy prophets."

Josefa called from the kitchen, "They are Mormons. They have plural wives."

Vati rose. "I'm a good Catholic and don't need any other religion."

Mutti, sitting next to Mr. Bishop, also rose. Her voice was cold. "There is no God. If there were, why would he allow all the misery I went through during the war?"

Mr. Ellis stood up, gathering the words he needed in German. "It's not God that caused this. It's the people. God has granted all of us free will, and that's what some chose to do with it."

That sounded wonderful to me. Now I understood that God loves us all, but he allows suffering in order not to interfere with our free will. I couldn't wait to think this over some more.

Mutti escorted my new friends to the door. "You have no idea of the suffering I went through. Thank you for your visit."

Mr. Ellis turned to Vati. "If your daughter is interested, could we return and tell her more?"

Mutti frowned, but Vati ignored her and said, "If she wants to, why not?"

I glanced from the Americans to Josefa and Carmen, who sat on the kitchen bench and giggled. They pointed their finger at their foreheads and made faces to indicate my stupidity. I turned my back to them but still saw their gestures in my mind. I wanted to sink into the floor. Nevertheless, I nodded. I wanted the two Americans to come and teach me, even if it meant more scoffs from my family. I knew that Jesus and God were real and loved me. And that seemed so much more important than what my family thought.

I accompanied the missionaries out the door. In front of our caravan steps, I found my voice. "I would like to learn more. You could come and talk to me in my small caravan."

Mr. Ellis took a small appointment book from his suit pocket. "That sounds great. Can we see you Thursday afternoon?"

We agreed on a time, and they went on their way. I stayed behind and watched them walk toward the Esso station, whose light framed them until they rounded a bend and I couldn't see them anymore.

I turned and wandered back to my home, wondering why I felt so light and excited. It seemed I had found something special and precious, and I was looking forward to learning more about it, even if that meant facing the opposition of my family. Let them think what they wanted; I would do what was right.

31

THE BOOK
OF MORMON

ON THURSDAY AFTERNOON, I MADE A FIRE IN THE SMALL CARAVAN and stayed there while my sisters went to the big home to be with the family. I kept looking out the window until I saw Mr. Ellis and Mr. Bishop come around the corner by the Esso station.

I opened the door and jumped down the steps to greet them, holding out my hand. "Hi, Mr. Ellis. Hi, Mr. Bishop. I was waiting for you."

They shook my hand and asked me to call them "Elder" instead of "Mister," since that was what missionaries were called.

Inside my little home, the elders sat on the sofa, and I pulled a chair close. They retold the story of Joseph Smith's search for the true church, and then they introduced me to the Book of Mormon. At the end of the lesson, Elder Ellis showed me a verse at the end of the book, in which Moroni urges the reader to ask God about the truth of the book and explains that God will let them know. The elders gave me a copy of the book for free, and they had even written a small note in it, referring back to Mormon's scripture.

As they rose, Elder Ellis asked me to come to church on Sunday. "We are meeting in the same classroom where we teach English," he said. "We would love to have you come and attend and learn more about God's restored Church."

What the elders told me resonated in my heart, and I assured them I would be there on Sunday.

Elder Ellis then told me what time services were, and, after making a new appointment for the next week, they shook my hand again and left.

As soon as they were gone, I settled down on the sofa and started reading the Book or Mormon. I started with the testimony of the witnesses at the very beginning, and their solemn declaration sunk into my heart. I related to the story of Nephi. Nephi and his family, just like mine, didn't have a permanent home. He too had to stand up for his faith against his siblings, as did I. When I finally stopped reading, it was dark, and my stomach was growling. Mutti called me to come eat. I sat among my siblings in the kitchen and hardly tasted my food. I kept thinking of Joseph Smith, who was the same age I was when he had his First Vision.

That night, as I lay in bed, I asked God to let me know whether the Book of Mormon and the Church were true. With a deep feeling of peace, I relaxed and fell asleep. I dreamed of a dark monstrous shadow chasing me on the Bachweide. It wouldn't let me get to my home. In my dream, I was afraid and prayed that God would protect me from the monster. As soon as I said my prayer, a tall man, a stranger to me, stepped from behind the caravan, brandishing a shiny sword. He stepped toward the monster and held the sword in front of him. The sword shot out beams of light from which the shadow quailed and finally dissolved. I felt completely safe and protected. The stranger in my dream turned to me and said, pointing to the sword, "This is the sword of the priesthood. It will protect you if you let it."

I woke and knew without a doubt that whatever these elders would tell me, it would be the truth.

A MAGICAL CHRISTMAS

ELSA, MEAGAN'S FRIEND, PICKS MEAGAN UP TO DO SOME SHOPPING. She smiles at Mutti, who, with bright eyes, sits on the sofa, watching the girls.

Meagan hurries down the steps from her bedroom, clutching her purse. "Let's go to the store around the corner. They always have good stuff."

"How about we go to the mall first?" I hear Elsa say as Meagan opens the door.

Meagan calls a cheery, "'Bye, Mom," and they are gone.

Mutti turns to me. "I don't understand a thing," she says. "Now, if they would speak Russian instead of English . . ."

I laugh. "Maybe if I had learned Russian that long ago, we'd be in Russia now."

"Oh goodness no. It's just as well you learned English. But that church thing that came with it . . . worried me."

I suppress a sigh. Mutti and I will never see eye to eye on that.

We watch the girls leave, still in animated discussion.

"I guess by now you know you didn't have anything to worry about," I say.

Mutti shakes her head and changes the subject.

DECEMBER 1961

I rose and stretched. It was Sunday morning. My breath formed a little puff of steam in the frigid air, but I hardly noticed it in my excitement. I pulled on a pair of the newfangled panty hose that had become so popular lately and slipped my prettiest blue dress over my head. Josefa and Carmen got up, put on their clothes, and disappeared into the warmth of the large caravan. I buttoned my sweater and stood in front of the mirror to tease my hair into a nice, fashionable pouf. With cold hands, I applied some lipstick and considered eye makeup but decided against it. Mutti would be mad if she noticed.

I left the little caravan and stepped across the platform into the warmth of the big one. The children sat around the kitchen table, chewing breakfast rolls. The smell of coffee wafted from the living room, where Mutti and Vati had their rolls.

Josefa quit talking to Franz and stared at me. "Sonja wants to go to church." She grinned.

I suppressed a sigh and sat on the corner of the bench.

Mutti called from the living room. "Just don't get too religious. You have to live in the world too."

I decided to ignore that and took another bite of my breakfast roll.

Soon the conversation turned to other things.

After breakfast, I rose, and eight-year-old Eva stood up at the same time. As I turned to the coat hook, she pulled my arm and asked, "What's church like?"

I smiled at her. "I don't know. You can go with me and we'll see."

"Okay."

She grabbed her coat from under Josefa's and followed after me.

Mutti called, "Where are you going with Eva?"

"I'm going to church. Eva wants to come with me."

Mutti frowned. "Okay, then. Just come home right after."

On that frosty morning, we marched the unpaved path to the bridge and walked along narrow cobblestone streets, through the shadow of the great gothic cathedral, to attend the small meeting.

Two families with a handful of young children and a few older people sat on the chairs in the classroom. We sang songs, said prayers, and listened to Elder Ellis talk in his accented German. An older lady interrupted several times in a loud voice for him to speak up.

In spite of the interruptions, I was ecstatic. This may have been a small congregation, but for me it was like coming home. No one here judged me. Unlike in the Catholic churches I attended when I was a child,

I understood what was happening, and I understood the language, since everybody spoke German and not Latin.

Elder Ellis talked about faith and how a person can grow his or her faith. He referred to a story from the Book of Mormon. I thought I was already developing faith and decided to read that part in the Book of Mormon as soon as I got home. I looked around at the small congregation. They believed it too and they would help me grow and develop my faith.

Eva fiddled with her hands but stayed quiet and polite.

At the end of the meeting, I took Eva's hand and smiled at some of the people. A black-haired girl with green eyes, about my own age, returned my smile. But I was too shy to approach anyone, and Eva pulled on my hand to go, so we left.

There was no hurry, I reassured myself. I would see them again. As we walked home, I hummed, "A Mighty Fortress," which we had sung as a closing hymn. I had a church to believe in, a place to go, and had met people who might become my friends. I thought of the suspicion I saw on most people's faces when they heard I was from the carnival, and I knew that here nothing would matter but our faith.

* * *

When I arrived at the train station, it was already dark. I spied Ursula, my new friend from church, and her parents. Her green eyes lit up when she saw me, and she smiled and waved. I rushed over and greeted her mother, who gave me a quick hug. Warmth suffused me in spite of the cold weather. Ursula and I chatted about the impending trip as we waited for the train.

Soon, most of the students from our English class had gathered, mixed in with many of the church members, about thirty or so people. The train arrived, and with a lot of excitement, we boarded for our trip to Giessen, where, as the missionaries had told us, we would visit the part of town where the American soldiers and their families lived.

On the short trip, I once again practiced the English words to "Silent Night" with Ursula, hoping I wouldn't forget them.

We walked from the train station to the army base's housing area, Ursula and I arm in arm. The guard talked to the missionaries and let us all through. We walked around the corner, and what I saw there made me forget to breathe. My eyes grew big in wonder.

In Germany, we used only white lights for Christmas, and no

Christmas decorations on private houses and buildings. But here the abundance of light and color saturated my eyes and my mind and exhilarated my soul. Tiny multicolored lights decorated the doors, eaves, and windows of the houses. Even the bushes in the yards radiated a riot of bright colors. Reflections of thousands of lights washed over the house fronts, the dormant lawns, and onto the sidewalk.

Brightly glowing figures of white and gold plastic angels, brown reindeer, and red, green, and white sleighs added to the strange sense of celebration the Americans seemed to have. I wondered if Mutti would consider these displays crazy and overdone. I shrugged. I liked them.

We sang at one house whose yard displayed two plastic reindeer decorated in green and red waves of light from the many small lights draped around the yard's trees and bushes. They pulled a sleigh from which a rotund Father Christmas waved at us, his cheery grin adding to the festive spirit of the season.

In my fascination, I forgot to be nervous about singing and especially about singing in English. Ursula and I stood between a gangly young man and a mother whose little girl stared at the display, her bright eyes peeking out from under her knitted hat and her mittened hands stuffed in her coat pockets. With enthusiasm, I joined the group in singing "Silent Night," my eyes still riveted on the colorful displays.

In the cold winter night, with our breath frosting the rims of our turned-up collars, we made our way through this strange winter wonderland, laughing, talking, and singing. Front doors opened wherever we went. People drifted onto their porches and front lawns to hear us. When we finished, they clapped and waved, and we went on to the next building.

Later, someone invited us into a larger hall, where smiling young American men and women served us hot chocolate topped with fluffy white puffs that dissolved into a sweet, sugary foam.

I had never before had so much fun, especially for a religious holiday. In my family, we celebrated Christmas, and only Christmas, by singing together. Except during that time, we never made any kind of music together. The four Sunday nights before Christmas, we observed Advent, the preparation for the birth of Christ. Mutti expected us to memorize and recite a Christmas poem for every Advent Sunday. We turned off the lights and lit one candle the first Sunday, then two, then three, and on the last Sunday before Christmas four candles shone brightly on the Advent wreath. In the glow of the candles, warmly enfolded by the dark, I felt safe and loved. After all the children recited their poems, we sang "Silent Night" or "Oh Come All Ye Children" or another one of the many popular German Christmas songs. I had always enjoyed the togetherness of our family for these celebrations, but they had been nothing compared to this.

To this day, when I hear "Silent Night" in English, I remember that winter and the warmth and magic my new church brought into my life.

33

NEW YEAR'S EVE

WE'RE AT AN ITALIAN RESTAURANT WITH MUTTI. KEN AND I order a diet soda, while Mutti peruses the wine list and then decides on a glass of water.

When the server is gone, Mutti says, "Good Italian food should be accompanied by wine. You still don't drink anything alcoholic, do you?"

"I don't," I say. "Juice or water is just as good."

"That little bit of alcohol won't make any difference," Mutti murmurs. "As I always say, everything in moderation is the way to go."

"You're right, but I make an exception with alcohol, Mutti. I still don't drink."

Our food arrives, and Ken asks Mutti if the Italian food in Germany tastes different than it does here. Soon they are in animated conversation, and I remember the first time my parents wanted me to drink alcohol.

NEW YEAR'S EVE 1961

I swooshed the dishrag around in the aluminum washbowl. "Can I celebrate New Year's with Ursula tonight?" I called through the open sliding door.

Mutti pulled a small sweater over a protesting Michael and let him toddle off. "Tonight you're not going to that church. You and Carmen are old enough to go with us to the town's New Year's Eve party. The mayor will be there."

I bit my lip to swallow a complaint. If I refused to go with my parents, then they would get angry, and I'd have to go anyway. And didn't God want us to be obedient to our parents? I simply had to suffer through the dumb party.

Josefa put another dried cup into the cupboard and called into the living room, "Why can't I go too?"

"You're too young," Mutti said. "You can go next year. Tonight I want you to tend Michael and Eva."

Josefa put away the last cup and gave me a nasty look. "You're too young too. They're just taking you because they don't want you to become a religious nut." She stormed into the living room.

Josefa was probably right. I had no business at that party. I didn't want to be displayed in front of the mayor and all the fat, red-faced, and complacent town councilors. Why couldn't Mutti let me go to the small celebration the youth at church planned?

Later, I put on my prettiest dress, experimented with makeup around my eyes, teased my hair, and drenched it with hairspray until it stood stiff in the shape I wanted. I was going to have fun if it killed me.

We arrived at the town hall, a large room decorated with streamers and colored paper, at about nine in the evening. At one end, a band sat with their instruments. The moving shadows of the guests, the waiters, and the dancers looked dark and unreal, like shadow puppets in the dim light. The whole scene seemed like the carnival halls with their brass bands and the happy, celebrating farmers and their wives.

I shot a longing glance at the doors we had just come through. A man in a suit, accompanied by a woman in a glittering yellow dress, followed us into the hall. Other people crowded in after them.

Vati found a table for us, and I gave up the thought of leaving. We sat and listened to people give speeches.

Vati ordered a bottle of champagne from the waiter, poured some into four glasses, and said, "You girls are big now. You can have some champagne tonight so you can properly toast the new year with us."

Carmen picked up her glass and took a sip. Her eyes grew wide. "I like it."

"Let's practice a toast," Vati said.

Mutti, Vati, and Carmen held up their glasses, waiting for me to pick up mine. But I didn't move. I crossed my arms over my chest. "I don't drink alcohol."

"What do you mean, you don't drink alcohol?" Mutti frowned.

"It's not good for you. And God doesn't want me to."

The smile disappeared from Vati's face. He set his glass back onto the table. "You mean the Mormons don't want you to."

My stomach cramped. So I was a religious nut. I didn't care how they saw me. I needed to do what God wanted me to do. I nodded, afraid to say anything else.

Mutti shook her head. "What shall we do with this dumb child?" she asked no one in particular.

"Can I have a soda?" I ventured.

"Why don't you drink your champagne? It has hardly any alcohol at all. And it tastes just like soda," Mutti said.

I shook my head.

"Oh, let her be," Vati said. He waved to a waiter and got me a soda.

"Okay. Now let's toast to the new year," he said and raised his glass.

Mutti and Carmen raised theirs, and after a moment's hesitation, I did the same with my soda. We clicked glasses, smiled at each other, and said "*Prosit*," the German toast.

Vati and Mutti sipped on their champagne, but Carmen emptied her glass in one long swallow, then took mine and drank it too. "Our Mormon chief doesn't drink alcohol," she said. "She probably thinks she's better than the rest of us. She's crazy."

I wished I were home in bed and under my covers. But I wasn't, so I balled my fists and ignored her. I knew I wasn't crazy. I had found the one true church, and if that meant I'd have to suffer through such labels, then so be it.

Mutti put down her glass. A red smear of lipstick on the rim seemed like a bloody smile. She shook her head in sorrow. "Just a little swallow wouldn't hurt. And you'd loosen up a little." She tried to pour some champagne into my soda.

I took my soda from the table and pretended to drink.

"At least try a sip," she said.

I felt like a freak, different from everyone around me, but I shook my head nevertheless. I trembled inside. To please God, I needed to be in the world but not of the world. I had always wanted to please Mutti, but now I had found a higher purpose, and that was more important to me than anything else.

Laughter and the clinking of glasses permeated the air. In the dim light, people gesticulated and hugged each other, talked, and ate. The smell of food mixed with the smell of cigarettes and alcohol and took me right back to the carnival beer tents. Didn't Mutti and Vati get enough of that in the summers? Why did we have to be here?

The band started up. I expected them to play brassy marches, like the bands in the beer tents, but they didn't. They played a waltz, "The Blue Danube."

People rose to dance. I was relieved when Vati asked Mutti to waltz with him. They couldn't badger me while they danced. I stayed seated and watched.

My parents made a lovely pair. My tall, white-haired father held Mutti, dressed in her low-cut midnight-blue dress, her black curls held back with a glittering clip. They danced so well, the crowd made room for them and watched. I watched too. This tall, elegant couple were so sure of themselves and their dancing. A warm gush of love washed over me. I was glad they were my parents. They were different from other parents; they were deeper, with more knowledge and understanding of the world. I thanked God in my heart I was born to them and not to other, more boring parents.

Later, after Vati danced with Carmen, he asked me to dance. He put his arm around my waist. The smell of his tobacco encircled us as he led me to the dance floor. I hadn't been that close to my father for as long as I could remember. I thought of Mutti dancing with him and knew I could never be that good.

I stiffened and stepped on his toes. Trying hard to place my feet right, I held myself like a rod. I had no idea what to do with my feet. Vati stopped and showed me the steps for the waltz, but still I tripped over my own feet and over his, my face burning with embarrassment.

Vati escorted me back to the table, returned to his chair, and turned to Mutti. "She needs to learn how to dance," he said.

A tall young man came to our table and asked if I wanted to dance, but heat coursed through my cheeks, and I shook my head. He then asked Carmen, and she danced with him. Carmen moved well to the music. I sat in my chair, sipping my soda, and tried to look as if I was having fun.

At the stroke of midnight, bells from churches all over town rang out in unison, singing their glad message of the old year gone and the new one begun. The distant sound of the train whistles joined them, and together with the solemn tolling of the bells and the joyous honking of the trains, the fireworks started. We pushed out of the doors with the rest of the crowd, lit our own sparklers, and watched the midnight sky light up with fireworks all over the city. The unending display of fireworks outshone the stars and even the moon, and I knew this coming year would be different and better for me than anything I experienced before.

34

THE CIRCUS

MUTTI AND I WATCH A GLITTERING, LAVISHLY COSTUMED TEAM OF acrobats seemingly fly through the air on "Cirque du Soleil" on TV. Mutti sighs.

"Things are so different now," she says. "Your father and I met in the circus. Those were hard times, but we were in love. I owe that to the circus."

"Do you remember when the circus came to Wetzlar in 1962?"

"I sure do. It was so much fun to see all my old circus friends again. But by then I had all of you to take care of, and I hardly had time for reminiscing."

When the circus came to Wetzlar that year, it was magical for me too.

MARCH 1962

One morning in March, I woke to the sound of heavy machinery chugging and people calling to each other on the usually quiet Bach-weide. I looked out the window. Three large tractors, one following the other, pulled a blue-and-white-painted circus caravan through the misty air into our quiet winter quarters. The name "Circus Althoff" was painted in red and yellow on several of the caravan wagons.

"What's going on?" Carmen moaned from her bed, her voice rough from sleep.

"Looks like a circus is coming. They're stationing their wagons right across from us."

Carmen jumped out of bed, and Josefa followed.

We dressed and hurried to the large caravan. I gulped down a piece of bread and some milk and went out to watch the spectacle. Josefa and Carmen rushed after me.

The tractor drivers encircled our small caravan with circus wagons. Soon, the circus roustabouts erected a fence all around the place, including our own caravan.

Throngs of people bustled about in our quiet winter quarters.

A tall older man, dressed in slacks and a blue shirt, came up to us girls. "Are you Margot Francesco's children?"

I folded my arms and nodded.

The door of our large caravan opened, and Mutti rushed out. "Bubi! How nice to see you!"

"Margot! How are you?" He held her at arm's length and looked her over, a big grin on his face.

My mouth fell open when he took Mutti's hand and kissed it. "We need a cashier. How about it? If you want a job, we'll take you back in a minute."

Mutti laughed. "I have plenty of work. But come on in. My husband, Kolya, is here too." She led Bubi into the caravan. We girls followed.

Vati shook Bubi's hand, and soon they were talking about horses and riding. Mutti served them breakfast and shooed us away. My sisters and I left to watch the roustabouts unroll a large canvas and put up the poles for the circus tent.

A few days later, the owner of the circus, a tall older woman named Carola, came to visit and reminisce with Mutti.

During that week, Mutti sometimes smiled at us for no reason. When little Eva came home from school, Mutti didn't give her the usual hard time about homework.

Wednesday afternoon, the circus opened for the first matinee. Mutti's circus friends gave us tickets to see the show for free. I had never before visited a real circus.

I sat wedged between my sisters on the bench in the big tent, at a loss for words. This wasn't at all like our carnival. All around us, people sat, rustling their programs. Circus employees trafficked in the aisles, selling candy and other items. The dark tent smelled of tobacco, sawdust, and horses. Somewhere from the shadows behind the rink, a brass band pumped out a waltz. The man Mutti had called Bubi rode into the ring on a gorgeous dark horse. He bowed to the audience, top hat in hand. His big smile made him look irresistible, like a prince.

Bubi showed off his horse. He made her stand still with a foreleg in the air, and then he rode at a gallop. While the horse galloped, Bubi slipped off the saddle, slid underneath the horse, and regained the saddle on the other side. After his performance, three beautiful women in glittering costumes and two slim men with big smiles climbed the ropes to the very top of the tent. I held my breath, afraid to move, hoping these brave people twirling through the air wouldn't tumble and fall.

Later I laughed with the crowd at the antics of the clowns and clapped in admiration when the trained dogs pulled each other in their cart, performed flips on command, and barked out a song. Elephants, monstrous and ponderous, circled the ring and held each other's tails.

Filled with cheers, laughter, and the bold sound of the circus band, the dark air engulfed me like a warm blanket. My Mutti had been part of this circus when she was young. She must have had a great and adventurous time. Maybe she would tell me more about her life in the circus.

When the matinee ended, I hurried to the caravan, full of questions. My siblings stayed to watch the caged animals of the circus menagerie.

Mutti stood in the kitchen, stirring soup in a pot and humming. I couldn't believe it. She hardly ever hummed or sang. I decided now was the time to ask my questions. "What did you do in the circus, Mutti? And how did you find it? Why did you go to the circus?"

I half expected her to brush me off, but she didn't. A faraway look settled in her eyes, and she sighed. "That was a long time ago, child," she began. "My mother had some money and considered herself higher society. She was mortified when I joined the circus." She stopped, turned the fire under the pot to low, and pulled a chair from the kitchen table.

I slipped into the converted bus seat while she sat on the chair. "Why did you join the circus?"

"I saw the poster on a wall. It just seemed to be a way out of all my trouble. I needed to get out of Berlin, and the circus was the perfect solution."

"Did you want to leave Berlin because of Hitler?"

"Yes. The Nazis were everywhere, and I knew sooner or later I would lose my job at the publishing company too. There were many reasons. But I did have fun in the circus."

"Did you meet Vati there?"

"I met your father when I worked in the circus that Müller had taken away from him."

Mutti told me about how she met Vati. I listened and forgot to breathe. What a strange life my Mutti had! She rarely talked about her life, but I knew she was half Jewish and hid from Hitler during the war. I watched my mother, still so beautiful, talk about a past that was surely more bitter than sweet, and decided I would one day write the story of her life.

The circus people who visited us never said a word about Hitler and the reason Mutti had worked in the circus, but now I knew. Mutti had left Berlin and her mother because things weren't good there for a dark-haired, half-Jewish girl.

The next day, I met some of my friends from church at the circus entrance. Together we went to the circus performance and enjoyed the festive atmosphere.

Later Ursula and I talked about a new band from England that had such great hits, like "Sie Liebt Dich" ["She Loves You"]. They were called the Beatles and were very popular in Germany at this time. The group would be going to America soon, and Ursula and I just knew they would be even more popular in the United States. We wished we could go too.

My mother and her past slipped from my mind in the excitement of what was happening in our teenage world.

My family enjoyed the thrill of the circus for two weeks, and then it left. We got ready for the next carnival circuit. But a few days later, our lives turned upside down again.

35

AN OPERATION

THE HOT SUNSHINE TURNS THE SAND ON THE OREGON BEACH INTO tiny particles of blistering heat. The cries of seagulls mingle with the happy shouts of the crowds. I blink into the bright sky. Mutti comes from the dressing rooms, wearing a black swimsuit. Her legs are strong and well formed, and she still has a nice figure. Together we wander across the sand, towels in our hands.

"You look great," I say. "No one would guess you're already over eighty. I hope I look that good when I am your age."

"I haven't been able to wear a bikini for a long time, like I used to, because of that scar," she says.

"What scar?"

"Remember how sick I was in 1962? Nowadays such operations leave hardly a mark, but back then I could have died."

Now I remember. How could I have forgotten my worry about Mutti?

APRIL 1962

I glanced out the window as I slipped into my brown everyday dress. The sun shone, and the trees along the fence displayed a lacy network of young, light green leaves. God had made the world so pretty. Once again, I thought about getting baptized. The missionaries had asked me several weeks ago, during the last lesson they had given me, whether I wanted to be baptized. With a big smile, I said, "Yes, I do. I have a testimony that the Church is true and that God wants me to be a member."

Elder Payne, who had replaced Elder Ellis, bent forward on the sofa in the small caravan. "Since you're so young, you need to have permission from your parents. Will you ask them for permission so we can set a date?"

The smile disappeared from my heart and my face. "I don't know. They really don't like me to be religious."

"The Lord will be with you and help you. Just go and ask."

I nodded. "Okay. But I'd better wait for the right moment."

And now, a month later, the moment still hadn't arrived. Every time I scraped up my courage to ask Mutti, I backed away at the last moment. And now it was almost too late. Soon we'd leave winter quarters, and when we would be traveling again, getting baptized would be impossible. I needed to do it now!

Suppressing a sigh, I followed Carmen across the platform to the large caravan. I expected a breakfast of fresh rolls, butter, and jam to be waiting, as usual. And this morning, even though my stomach made a flip and my knees went weak, I was determined to ask Mutti about my getting baptized.

But when I entered the kitchen, the table was empty. My sudden relief at the postponement of my urgent question for Mutti was tinged with disappointment. I shook off both feelings. What was going on?

"Carmen, make breakfast for the children," Vati called from the living room. "Mutti is sick. She'll stay in bed today."

Mutti was sick? I couldn't remember a time when she was sick enough to stay in bed. My worry about myself and my baptism disappeared and was replaced with worry about my mother. I glanced into the living room. The sofa was still out, and Mutti lay on it, the feather quilt pulled up around her shoulders.

"It's just a stomachache," she said. "I'll feel better soon. In the meantime, you big girls will have to keep things going."

While Carmen sliced the bread and spread margarine on it, I dressed Michael.

A sudden cry from the sofa froze the squirming Michael. "Mutti! Mutti!" he cried, and a moment later, he escaped my hands and climbed onto Mutti's bed.

Mutti screamed.

I grabbed Michael by the legs and pulled him off the bed.

"Are you all right, Mutti?" Carmen called from the kitchen.

"Keep that kid away from me, Sonja!"

"I'm sorry," I said. I grasped Michael around the middle. He wriggled and squirmed, trying to get free. "He just escaped."

Mutti lay stiffly in bed and sighed. "It's not so bad if I don't move. It will probably go away again."

But as the day wore on, she cried out more often, and soon she didn't dare move at all. I kept the two little ones quiet in the small caravan, my mind on Mutti. In spite of my fervent hopes that she would soon feel better, her condition got worse every time I checked on her. Eva and Michael played quietly, occasionally asking about Mutti.

"She'll be all right soon," I told them, but my eyes smarted from holding back the tears. I kept praying in my heart for Heavenly Father to make her feel better. When I checked on her later that afternoon, she was trying to get up.

"Don't move, Mutti," Carmen said, her voice small and shaky. "It will just hurt again."

"I have to go to the bathroom." With a cry of pain, Mutti sank back into the bed.

Vati shooed all of us out. Together we huddled in the little caravan, exchanged fearful looks, and hoped Mutti would be okay.

The early sunshine of the day seemed dimmer, and even the waving of the branches on the trees stilled as if they too held their breath.

Vati came from the caravan. He supported a bent-over Mutti wrapped in her black winter coat.

"I'm taking her to the doctor," Vati said. "Carmen, take care of things."

Mutti grimaced in pain, and she breathed in hard gasps. Vati half carried, half dragged her to our the blue station wagon that had replaced our VW the year before, and soon we watched it go around the corner onto the bridge.

Vati returned several hours later, without Mutti.

"She has gallstones," he answered our anxious questions. "She's in the hospital. Tomorrow they'll operate and get them out. She will be back in a few days."

A burden fell off my shoulders. She would be all right. God had heard my prayers.

Once again we were motherless. The caravan seemed quieter, less crowded, without Mutti.

The night after the operation, Vati went to see Mutti. When he returned, a worried chorus of "How is she?" greeted him.

Vati closed the door and smiled. "Mutti is doing fine. The doctors said she can come home in a few days."

Josefa and I exchanged a shaky smile. Eva hugged Michael, who chanted, "Mutti, Mutti."

Carmen turned from the stove, where she was cooking chicken soup. "Can we visit her?"

"Not yet. An operation is a hard thing, and Mutti needs her rest. But you can visit her before she comes home."

And we did. Two days later, all six of us children squeezed into Vati's station wagon, and Vati drove us up the hill to the hospital.

Mutti lay in a room with two other sick people. Her black hair shone on the white pillows, and her skin was almost as pale as the sheets. She smiled when she saw us. "My stomach hurts. But I feel a lot better. At least now I can move without pain."

She showed us the gallstones the doctors had removed from her body. We six children crowded around and stared at the dark stones on the waxed paper in her hand.

When Michael started to squirm, Carmen took him outside to walk in the hallway. Josefa and Eva trailed after her. Franz went to the bathroom, and for a moment I was alone with my parents. Mutti smiled at me.

She looked happy and relaxed, as if she had already recovered. I patted her hand and felt now was the moment to ask what had been on my mind for so long. Maybe, having been so sick, Mutti might not mind.

"Can I be baptized?" I asked. "I really want to."

Mutti's smile vanished. She searched my face. "You're serious about that church?"

I nodded.

Mutti turned to Vati and said, "What shall we do with this child?"

"I don't like it. It's a sect, not a church. Why can't she be Catholic, like me?"

"Please, Vati," I said. "They teach me what's right. And they pray to God, just like the Catholics."

"Is that what you really want?" Vati said.

I nodded.

Mutti looked at me, a frown of worry on her face. "Let's wait one year. If you still want to be baptized by the end of next winter quarters, you can."

"I don't like it," Vati grumbled.

My heart grew lighter. I had been sure both my parents would say no. This was much better. I could easily wait a year, and at least now I had her promise.

Mutti turned her head to Vati. "Just wait. By next year, she'll have forgotten all about it."

The door burst open, and my sisters followed Michael into the room. I didn't say anything to Mutti's statement, but in my heart I vowed I never would forget about being baptized. I would always do what Heavenly Father wanted me to do.

36

ONE LAST SUMMER

MUTTI AND I WALK PAST AN LDS MEETINGHOUSE. MUTTI squints at it. "Seems like you have churches everywhere."

I smile. "As you can see, it doesn't keep people from living a normal life."

Mutti frowns and walks on, and I hurry to catch up. She slows and turns to me. "I was so worried about you when you were a teenager. I'll never forget the stunt you pulled on your fifteenth birthday."

I still feel a twinge of guilt when I think back to that day. "I didn't mean to worry anyone. And, as you found out, there really was no reason to get upset."

That summer I wanted to do what's right and make God proud of me, but somehow things didn't turn out quite right.

SUMMER 1962

At the end of May, we started the carnival season with the spring festival in Wetzlar, then went on to Biskirchen, where we ran our attractions in the first week of June every year. More than ever before, I wished I wouldn't have to travel or work on Sundays. With the first money I made, I went to a bookstore and bought a Bible to go with my Book of Mormon and the Doctrine and Covenants the missionaries had given me for a good-bye present. I vowed I'd read the scriptures every day.

In July, we stayed a week in a tiny town by Wetzlar, called Niederbiel, then we moved on to the beautiful old university city of Limburg.

Fantastic stone gargoyles sat like guardians on the girders of an old stone bridge and watched the slow traffic across the bridge and the narrow, crooked cobblestone streets. The bustle of the university students who visited our attractions was different from the usual crowds. I watched these older teens and wished I could go to a university too. Since I couldn't, I went home to the small caravan, took out my Bible, and read a few chapters.

During that summer, I was busy every Sunday, since Josefa and I ran our own small attraction. I satisfied myself with reading the scriptures whenever I could. The missionaries received permission to write me one letter a month. I lived for those letters and news from my small branch in Wetzlar.

The end of September, when our route took us to Aschaffenburg, another lovely old town, I decided to find a branch of The Church of Jesus Christ of Latter-day Saints. In Aschaffenburg, we weren't supposed to open for business on Sunday until after noon, and that worked out perfectly, since that Saturday, the twenty-ninth, I celebrated my fifteenth birthday, and I wanted to celebrate it by going to church the next day.

On Saturday, my birthday, I walked to one of the yellow phone booths dotting the inner city around the marketplace and searched for a listing for the Church. I found the listing and copied the address.

Sunday morning, I put on my best dress and combed my hair. I took off on my bike to find the church at about a quarter to nine, without telling anyone. As I rode deeper into the city center, I stopped to ask for the street where the church members would meet, but I couldn't find it. At about ten, I leaned my bike against an old Protestant church and entered to sit in the back and simply feel the spirit of the people who were attending the service. On that cold wooden bench, in spite of the chill in the air and apart from the rest of the congregation, I felt at peace and at home. This was my birthday, and I had started it with God as my companion, maybe not the way I wanted, but I knew Heavenly Father had been pleased with my earnest search.

With the last "Amen," I remembered my family and slipped out. I pedaled home as fast as I could, trying to still my conscience.

They never miss me, so why should they now? I reassured myself as the wind whipped the hair from my face. I hoped I could slip into the small caravan as if I'd never been gone, and things would go on as normal. It was only eleven, plenty of time to get ready for business. I didn't want to explain that I had gone to find a branch of the Church.

I jumped from the bike, leaned it against the side of the caravan, and hurried in.

Mutti faced Vati in the kitchen. She turned and saw me.

Her lips tightened, and her look was icy. I shivered and hugged myself.

Josefa, on the bench at the table, pointed at me. Her voice dripped with righteous accusation. "Here she is."

Mutti snarled at Josefa. "I can see that." Turning to me, relief softened the anger in her voice. "Where have you been? You didn't have an accident, did you? We were ready to have the police look for you."

My good spirits left with the breath escaping my mouth. I hung my head, knowing I had disappointed my family once again. "I'm sorry. I should have said something."

Vati strode up to me. "And where, exactly, did you go without telling anyone?"

I stared onto the floor. "I went to church," I mumbled.

"And for *that* you had us all worried? How stupid is that? It's dangerous out there. Something could have happened to you."

Mutti stepped closer to me. "Did you even stop to think about the trouble you caused? You know you're not allowed to go anywhere without telling us. We didn't know what to think."

My eyes stung. I wanted to sink into the ground.

Vati turned to Mutti. "Leave the child be. Nothing happened to her."

Mutti stared at Vati, then back at me. She shrugged. "At least you're back safely. That's all that matters. Happy birthday."

Vati turned to get his jacket from the hook. "Let's open the attractions. It's getting time."

Carmen and Josefa stared at me as I hurried past them and into the small caravan to change clothes and get ready for work.

Later that evening, after we closed the attractions at about eleven, Vati beckoned for us girls to come into the large home before going to bed. He presented me with an extra gift for my birthday, a gold necklace with a green stone held in place by a golden wire. His arms reached around me to close the clasp on my neck. I breathed in the familiar scent of cigarettes that always surrounded him. Vati closed the clasp, smiled, and stepped back. I returned his smile, grateful that we were all here together and that my world was whole.

At the end of October, we returned to Wetzlar for their autumn festival and then moved across the bridge back to the Bachweide for winter quarters.

37

THINGS ARE CHANGING

MY EIGHTEEN-YEAR-OLD DAUGHTER, LIESEL, LEAVES WITH HER boyfriend to go to a movie.

Mutti and I glance through the window after her. We watch as Liesel takes his hand.

Mutti turns to me and sighs. "It was so hard raising all you girls when you were young," she says. "Vati and I had to watch out for you all the time, especially when the boys gathered around."

"Now that I'm a mother myself, I can see that it wasn't easy for you," I say. "Times were so different then."

I change the subject and ask Mutti what she wants for supper. But I still remember the boys in the different towns. Mostly they were crude and made innuendoes I didn't quite understand. I didn't like them, but I liked the attention they gave me.

Now I understand what Mutti went through with three teenage daughters on the carnival circuit every year. Thinking back to the winter of 1962–63, I also understand what Mutti and Vati's argument had been all about.

MUTTI AND DAUGHTERS

OCTOBER 1962

The first Sunday after arriving in Wetzlar, I attended church in the rooms the branch had rented not far from the train station. The branch had grown, and we now had a local branch president instead of the missionaries. A young man, a member of the Church from southern Germany, had married a local girl who had converted to the gospel while I was gone. Another family with children and two older ladies with two of their grandchildren had also joined the Church. Ursula was delighted to see me again, and we picked up our friendship as if I hadn't been away at all.

Instead of going to the youth center, I now spent all my time with my LDS friends or in church, but I still visited the library and read as voraciously as before.

One cold evening, I sat in the warm kitchen, reading a book from the library. Franz, Michael, and Eva were already in bed, and Josefa and Carmen were in the small caravan. I wanted to read a bit longer before I followed them. The oven in the small caravan was probably out, anyway, and here warmth enveloped me.

"It isn't right for a wife not to be with her husband," I heard Vati grumble from the living room.

My heart constricted and turned into a small lump. I stopped reading and listened. What were Vati and Mutti talking about? Did Mutti want to leave again? From the living room, Mutti spoke. "The girls are getting bigger. Don't tell me you haven't seen the boys hovering around them."

"They have good sense. They'll be okay."

"I've seen Sonja flirt. I wonder what else could happen."

I shrank into my corner. They must have forgotten I was still here. *Flirting,* I thought. *I'm just friendly to those boys. I don't flirt.*

"We'll just have to watch them," Vati said.

"What about Eva? She needs a more steady life. She isn't doing well in school now, and with her not able to attend summer school regularly, she'll fall behind more and more. Franz would do better in school too."

Vati sighed. "I don't like it."

"Why can't we have it like the Fehtzes? They live in an apartment in the winter. In the summer Herr Fehtz runs his carnival, and Frau Fehtz and the children travel to where he puts up his attractions and help. The children have a more steady life, not being on the road all the time."

"It's almost impossible to get an apartment nowadays," Vati said.

"You'd have to be on a waiting list. Remember Antje's family? They waited for over a year."

I got goose bumps. An apartment! That would be so nice. Our family would have much more room, and surely I could somehow get my parents to let me stay home on Sundays. I could go to church, and my sisters could work the attractions. They would be happy because they could keep their share of the money, and I would be happy because I wouldn't have to be at the carnivals anymore.

I turned in my seat and my knee banged against the wall.

Mutti's voice rose. "Is that you, Carmen?"

Darn! Now they'd surely send me out. But there was no helping it. "No, it's me."

"What are you still doing here? Get into your own caravan. Now."

I grabbed my book and ran out.

An apartment in Wetzlar! The possibilities this opened up! I hardly slept that night. It meant that I would be close to my church all the time. And maybe I could even get permission to get baptized. I hadn't dared reminding Mutti of her promise yet. But everything seemed possible that night.

As winter wore on, I heard nothing more about a possible apartment, but things were changing, nevertheless.

33

WORK

LIESEL AND MEAGAN BURST INTO THE KITCHEN, WHERE MUTTI and I finish loading the dishwasher.

"Can we have some money?" Liesel asks. "Elsa is coming over, and we want to go to the dollar store."

"Okay," I say and dig ten dollars out of my wallet. "Bring me some paper towels too."

The girls disappear with the money. Mutti watches them. "What a drain today's teenagers are on their families. When I was their age, I contributed to the family's upkeep."

"At least you completed an apprenticeship in that fancy store and even modeled fashions. I didn't get to do anything like that."

"What else could I have done when you were young? You girls couldn't have finished apprenticeships, with us having to travel in the summer. And by the time you were older, the country had recovered from the war and was in an economic upswing. It had been easy for me to get work for you and Carmen without you having to go through a long and nonpaying apprenticeship first."

I think back. "Even so, my first job away from the carnival was exciting."

NOVEMBER 1962

One morning at breakfast, Mutti said, "Eva, get going or you'll be late for school."

Eva buttoned her coat, grabbed her satchel, and slammed the door on her way out.

Mutti turned to me. "Sonja, Josefa, watch Michael. And don't fight. Carmen, you're coming with me."

Vati rose from his breakfast and frowned at Mutti. His eyes were hard, and I thought he looked unhappy. He went outside with sloped shoulders, the smoke of the cigarette in his mouth trailing after him.

For the last few weeks, Vati had been rebuilding the pack trailer. He broke out the back and added a section, inserted two windows, and built a partition, which separated the packed attractions from the new section.

Now he went to work on that caravan. He didn't seem interested in what Mutti did with Carmen.

Carmen, already all dressed up and with her hair poufed and sprayed, said, "What if they don't like me?"

Mutti shrugged into her black winter coat and grabbed her purse. "Don't worry. I already talked to the owner. They want to give you a try." With Carmen in tow, she left our home and walked along the dirt road and across the bridge. Two hours later, she returned, a satisfied smile on her face.

At six that evening, Carmen returned home.

Mutti smiled broadly at her, and we children surrounded her in a cluster.

"How was it? Was it fun?" Josefa asked.

With shiny eyes, Carmen told us about her first day at work and how much she liked it. "Mr. Meier said I work really well. He's glad he has me."

Since she had never had an apprenticeship, Carmen worked as a "gopher" or "girl Friday" at Meier's printing company. She carried papers, books, and other items from one office to another, made coffee, and did whatever needed to be done.

A week later, Mutti returned from a walk to town. She took off her coat and turned to me, her cheeks still rosy from the cold air outside and a smile on her face. "I've applied for you to work at Leitz. They need factory workers. They said for you to come tomorrow morning at eight. You'll make 1.76 deutschmarks an hour. That will help feed you all."

For once, I was speechless. It never occurred to me that I would have to go out and work too. After all, I was so much younger than seventeen-year-old Carmen—almost two years! Why couldn't I stay home like last winter? I had my church and the youth meetings there, and I had my friends from church. On the other hand, I reconsidered. If Mutti thought I was old enough to work, she might also let me be baptized. I hadn't brought up the subject yet since she disliked me going to my meetings so much. This might be the perfect time to ask. But something held me back even though I had promised the missionaries I'd remind her of the promise she had made me last winter.

Instead, I thought of getting paid. "Do I get to keep some of the money I make?"

"You can keep twenty Deutschmarks from each paycheck," Mutti said.

That sounded good. It was about as much as Vati let us have last summer when we worked our attraction. With my first paycheck, I'd buy one of those small transistor radios that were so popular.

But what if I didn't know how to work in a factory? I frowned at Mutti. "What will I have to do?"

"I don't know. They'll show you tomorrow. Don't worry. They'll make sure you understand."

"Okay." I hoped Mutti was right.

The next morning, Mutti rose early and walked with me to the other side of the bridge to the large Leitz building. She took me to the manager and left.

At Leitz, I learned to sort and weigh screws. It was easy work, and the people I worked with were all older.

Hilda was one of the women I sometimes talked to during breaks. One day, we came to the subject of race. Hilda sat next to me in the break room, finishing a cup of coffee. She told me about her only son, who was still in school.

"He's a good kid," she said. "He's a real German. I'm proud of him."

"What do you mean, 'a real German?'" I asked.

She bent closer and lowered her voice.

"Hitler may have done a lot wrong," she confided. "But he was right about one thing. All the misery we went through during the war, it was all the Jews' fault. If it wasn't for the Jews, things would be different here in Germany."

I thought of my Mutti and the way she hid in the circus, just because her father had been Jewish. Hilda couldn't possibly be a better person than my Mutti. Hilda didn't have to hide from the Nazis, but that didn't make her superior.

"So, if your son wanted to marry a person who has Jewish ancestry, you wouldn't let him?"

"I'd never speak to him again," she said.

I looked her straight into the eyes. "Do you think I'm a nice person?"

"You're a bit young, but you have a good head on your shoulders. You're okay."

"I wonder if it would make any difference to you, if you knew that I'm partly Jewish myself?"

Hilda stared at me, her mouth wide open. She scooted away from me on the bench.

"You're joking, right?"

"No, my mother is half Jewish. That's why I grew up in a carnival. She hid in a circus to get away from the Nazis."

Hilda finished her coffee with great gulps, got up, and never again took her break at the same time I did. In fact, she never talked to me again.

39

VATI AND MUTTI AT ODDS

WE'RE GETTING READY FOR THE OUTDOOR CONCERT AT THE PARK. Mutti and I situate ourselves on the grass while Ken gets us drinks. Mutti watches him at the concession stand, patiently standing in line behind a heavy young woman and her two children. "You did right with him, child," she says. "He treats you nice." She sighs. "Your father changed. We had so much fun when we were younger. But after Michael's birth, he was always angry. Nothing I did made him happy."

"Is that why he built living quarters into the pack trailer?"

"He couldn't understand why I wanted to quit traveling with him. You girls were growing up, and the carnival life wasn't safe for three teenage girls. He didn't like it, but I had to insist. His attitude just made things easier."

After having raised my own daughters, I understand why Mutti wanted to quit traveling. But at the time I mainly felt scared and worried.

DECEMBER 1962

Darkness descended before I got home from work. I strode across the bridge, entered the small caravan, and hung up my coat. My breath formed little puffs of steam in the frigid air. The stove was cold, as it now always was, since Carmen and I weren't home during the day.

It had been a long time since lunch, and my stomach growled. It was almost six, and supper should have been on the table by now. Maybe Mutti had made potato leek soup with our usual supper sandwiches.

Saliva collected in my mouth, and I swallowed in anticipation. Maybe she made oxtail soup. That would taste great too.

I hurried across the platform into the anticipated comfort of the big caravan and opened the door. A rush of warmth greeted me. But the gas range, pushed away from the wall, obstructed my view. I squeezed around it and almost collided with Mutti's backside, which protruded from behind the stove.

A math book, a notebook, and two pencils littered the kitchen table. Eva sat squeezed in the corner of the bench, writing on a paper. The gas range was off, and it seemed no one had thought of supper. The place smelled like propane gas. My stomach, already empty, threatened to turn over.

The noise of metal hitting metal came from behind the stove. "I'll show him," Mutti grumbled. "I've had about enough of this."

I knew better than to bother Mutti when she was in such a mood. Without making a sound, I tiptoed into the living room, where Michael and Josefa sat on the sofa.

"What's happening?" I whispered.

Josefa rose, gave Michael a warning look, and motioned me to follow her. In the small caravan, she pulled a chair away from the table and sat. "We ran out of gas for the stove. Mutti asked Vati to disconnect the old propane bottle and put on a new one. Vati was really mad. He told Mutti that if she wanted to cook something, she should rub her hands under the pot until it got warm. He wasn't going to do anything for her and her darned children."

My heart sank. Vati didn't get mad a lot, but when he did, his words made me feel as if I had no father. More and more often during this winter, Vati acted as if we weren't his children. I shivered in the cold caravan and hugged myself. My thoughts returned to Mutti and the missing supper.

"Now she's trying to change that monstrous gas tank herself?" I asked.

"Yes, and she's boiling mad. Vati is sitting in his half-finished caravan apartment, ordering Franz around, and eating antacid pills. But he didn't come to help."

"I'm cold," I said. Josefa stood and we slunk back into the large caravan, where Mutti still worked behind the range.

Finally, Mutti stood up, and we helped her push the range back against the wall. Carmen came in from her job, and Mutti told us to make some sandwiches.

"I bought some bologna if there's not enough to make butter and jam sandwiches," she said. "I have to clean up."

We finished eating, and I was washing the few dishes when Vati stormed in.

"Where's my supper?" he demanded.

"Make it yourself," Mutti said. "And don't turn on the burners. I'm not sure I hooked the gas up right."

"Darn children," Vati grumbled and pushed the range out again. A few minutes later, he pushed it back in and scowled at Mutti. "Make me some soup. It's cold out there."

Without another word, Mutti put a pot onto a burner, and Vati had his soup that evening. We kids were quiet as mice around the caravan that evening, and we went to bed early.

When I returned from work the next day, Mutti was gone, and no supper waited for us. My heart plummeted when I noticed her absence. The stove in the living room put out welcome heat, and Vati sat on the sofa, sipping a cup of coffee.

"Where's Mutti?" I mouthed to Josefa. She stared at me and shrugged. I was opening the bread box on the counter opposite the kitchen table, ready to make some sandwiches, when the door opened and Mutti came in, followed by Carmen and a blast of cold air.

"Where were you?" Vati asked.

"I'm going to make supper," Mutti said. "Sonja, slice the bread." She rummaged in her shopping bag and pulled out a package of lunchmeat. "Josefa, get out the plates."

Vati didn't say anything else, and the tension in the air drained. Soon we all sat together around the kitchen table, eating sandwiches and sipping our hot drinks.

On Saturday, Vati received a letter. He came in and waved the opened letter in the air. "Margot," he said, "I got a letter from a lawyer. Do you know anything about that?"

Mutti stopped reading her book and stared at him, lips pressed together. "When you refused to help with the gas tank, that was the last straw," she said. "If I have to be the mother in the home and do your job too, I might as well live on my own. I'm getting a divorce."

We children huddled together in front of the television Vati had bought for the family at the end of the summer. No one watched it. We stared at each other instead. A divorce? What would happen to us?

My worst fears had come true. I stared at Vati, expecting an outbreak similar to the ones he used to have after Mutti came home from wherever she went a few summers ago.

Vati didn't move. He looked at Mutti with quiet eyes and said, "If you don't want me anymore, then I don't want you either."

He took his letter and left. His heavy steps reverberated through the caravan. I fled to the small caravan, crawled into bed, and buried my face in my pillow. Now Vati was leaving us. But at least we had Mutti.

I cried, not sure for what. Eventually I drifted off to sleep.

Within the week, Vati had built a bed into the new addition to the pack trailer. After that, he only came to our home when one of us children called him for supper.

* * *

On a Saturday afternoon a few days later, I caught Mutti alone. She was sitting on the sofa, reading a book. I had the strongest feeling that the time was right, so I came closer. Mutti looked up.

I took a deep breath. "Do you remember what you promised me last year, Mutti?"

"No. What?"

I shifted my weight from one foot to the other. "You'd let me be baptized this winter if I still wanted to."

Mutti was quiet.

"Can I be baptized? I still want to."

Mutti glanced through the living room window, probably at Vati's caravan, shook her head, and turned back to me. "I don't like it. You know that. But since you're so set on it, go ahead. Vati can't say anything about it now, or I'll use it in my divorce complaint. After all, the law allows you to choose your religion after you're fourteen." She sounded satisfied somehow.

My body relaxed. "Thank you."

I was happy. Even though the divorce was a bitter and scary thing, Heavenly Father had used it to make it possible for me to get baptized. And I got that permission without another fight. Mutti hadn't even put down the Church. I realized that in God's hands even something bad can become a good thing.

I was baptized by immersion in a Frankfurt church building on December 16, 1962. My friend Ursula and her family were there, but no one from my family was. I don't think my sisters even knew what I was doing that afternoon.

40

MUTTI MAKES A DECISION

W'ERE VISITING AN INDOOR MALL. MUTTI MARCHES ALONG, checking out the wares in the windows. A small gift store reminds me of one of the stores in downtown Wetzlar.

"I remember all the tiny stores in Wetzlar," I say. "Carmen told me they took out the cobblestones and made the downtown area a pedestrian zone."

"I don't know about that. I never really liked it in Wetzlar. But for a while, when I quit traveling with your father, it seemed to be a fine, big city. I was happy even though we still lived in the caravan."

"I think Franz wanted to stay with us too," I say.

"Maybe he did, and maybe he didn't," Mutti says. "But I couldn't just let your father go off all alone, without any help. And Franz was the one he relied most on. So I let him have his son."

I hear the defensive note in Mutti's voice and say nothing. She *must* have noticed Franz shaking his head that morning in 1963.

FEBRUARY 1963

I rose in the early morning darkness. My breath condensed on my lips and nose. I turned on the light and, with goose bumps already forming on my arms, slipped from my flannel nightgown into the dress and cardigan I had laid out the night before. The big caravan was probably still warm, and I looked forward to a piece of bread and a cup of hot chocolate before going off to work.

I opened the door and squinted. The overhead light bulb blazed in the kitchen. Vati sat on a chair in front of the kitchen table, a lit cigarette in his hand. I was surprised to see my brother up too. Twelve-year-old Franz sat in my corner of the kitchen bench, still in his pajamas. His blond hair stood on end. He looked at me and dropped his gaze. His eyes were red and shiny—from sleep, I thought.

I went to the counter and sliced myself a piece of bread.

Vati didn't acknowledge me. He looked at Mutti, who was leaning against the open living room door, wrapped in her powder-blue house-coat, disheveled dark hair around her pale face.

"I can't do all the work by myself," Vati said to her. "I need the kids to help me."

I turned to get the margarine from the kitchen table.

Mutti crossed her arms in front of her chest and tapped her foot. Her voice was sharp. "I told you. You can have Franz. I even woke him up for you. Take him and leave me alone."

Franz stared at Mutti. He shook his head no, but Mutti ignored him, and Vati did too. They would have, even if they saw him do it. Mutti and Vati expected us to do as we were told.

The door opened. Carmen entered, followed by a rush of cold air.

No one noticed Carmen. It seemed as if we children were ghosts, pawns in a private war fought between my parents.

"I need the girls," Mutti said. "How do you expect me to live with that tiny bit of alimony and child support you'll pay? I need their income to survive."

I thought of Vati. He needed the girls, he said, but I didn't want to work in the carnival anymore. I couldn't think of any other way to help him. I was glad Mutti wanted us, and at the same time, I wished I hadn't been born. Then Vati wouldn't need me or miss me.

As always, we children pretended everything was normal. I spread jam on my piece of bread and turned to the cupboard over the counter, rummaging for a cup.

"I'll help you on the weekends, Vati," Carmen said. "I'm going to get my driver's license. Then I'll buy a car and go wherever you are in the summers and help."

"I'll let you have twenty percent of everything you make," Vati said, relief coloring his voice.

I bit my lip. I wanted to help Vati, but I hated the carnival. And I did not want to give up my Sundays. I loved Heavenly Father and wanted to do what he expected of me. Working on Sundays wasn't right. If Carmen worked with Vati on the weekends, and Franz lived with him, he'd have enough help. Maybe Josefa would go with Carmen too. I quietly set the kettle onto the burner for my cocoa water to heat.

* * *

MARCH 1963

I hurried up the stairs into the caravan, glad to be done with another day of work.

"Guess what?" Josefa greeted me. Without another breath, she went on, "Mutti and Vati went to the judge today, and their divorce is final. Mutti is out buying a new dress to celebrate."

The rattle of Carmen's new Karmann Ghia Volkswagen interrupted her. The car's engine stopped, and footsteps came up the steps. Mutti entered, followed by Carmen.

Mutti put her shopping bag on the table. "Josefa, now that you're done with school, I got you a job too," she said. "You'll be working for Atwoods, the British architecture firm." Mutti smiled as if nothing else mattered. "You'll love it there. Get ready tomorrow by eight, and I'll take you there."

Josefa started working, and not much else changed, except that Vati built a second bedroom in his pack trailer, and when it was finished, Franz moved in.

41

AT THE CARNIVAL AGAIN

W E SIT AT THE KITCHEN TABLE, OLD PHOTOS SPREAD OUT IN front of us. I glance through the glass doors at the summer rain while Mutti looks at a photo of a teenage me in the ball toss booth Vati had built for us girls. In it, I lean against one of the posts, selling balls to a customer. I'm wearing my favorite hot pink jacket over a pair of dress pants.

"One of my friends from church took that picture," I said. "That was the spring festival in Finsterloh by Wetzlar, the first time the family didn't run the carnival together. You and Vati were divorced then. We girls helped Vati run the attractions, but you never came."

"I had Eva and Michael. They were still little, and it would have been a hassle to take the bus that far with them. So I stayed home and enjoyed my first weekend in years and years without everybody there."

And I once again ran a carnival attraction without wanting to, but without complaining.

SONJA IN THE BALL TOSS BOOTH

MAY 1963

I walked across the bridge and admired the shiny green leaves on the trees. The sunshine warmed my back. When I turned onto the path toward our caravan, I noticed something was different. The tractor, our car, and Vati's pack trailer were gone. Our two homes were hunkered in their space next to the fence, all by themselves. They looked small and lost in the big, empty space.

I climbed the four steps onto the platform. The doors stood open to let in the sunlight.

I came in, shrugging out of my unbuttoned coat.

Eva looked up from her math book. "Vati moved his caravan to Finsterloh while you were working. They have their spring festival this weekend."

For a moment Eva's words made no sense, and then I realized the carnival season had started, and we weren't going to travel with Vati. My heart grew lighter at the thought.

I went to the small caravan, put down my purse, and plopped onto my bed, thinking. Vati would be without us during the summer. I wondered if he would be all right. At least for his first week of the season, we were close. Carmen could be in Finsterloh in less than ten minutes with her new car. Josefa would probably love to go with her too. Then Vati wouldn't need me.

When Carmen and Josefa arrived home from work, I returned to the big caravan. Mutti fed us liverwurst sandwiches and chicory coffee. "You girls, hurry and finish your supper," she said. "I want you to go over to the festival grounds and help your Vati."

My stomach clenched. I swallowed and put my sandwich onto the plate. "Do I have to go?"

Carmen sighed. "Don't you want to make the extra money? Vati said he'll give us twenty percent of the intake, double what we made last summer."

"Wow!" Josefa said. "With the money Mutti lets us keep from our daily job, we'll be rich. I can't wait. I want to buy a Beatles record."

I didn't care about the money. At least not that much. But if I had to help anyway, I might as well take the extra cash. Maybe I'd buy a record too of Johnny Cash and his American music.

After we ate, Carmen invited us to ride in her new car over to Vati's. We arrived at the carnival grounds just a few minutes later.

Vati greeted us, face drawn and eyes red-rimmed. He nodded at us and said, "Sonja and Josefa, you'll put up and run the ring attraction. Carmen, you and Franz set up the shooting gallery. Franz, when that's done, come and help with the merry-go-round. Let's get going. Time is short."

* * *

Saturday morning, Carmen hurried us to get ready so we would be at the fairgrounds before Vati opened the attractions. The merry-go-round stood all ready for business in the large, grassy area of the Finsterloh exhibition. Mickey Mouse and Donald Duck, with his three nephews, grinned at the crowds from the pictures in the center and on the roof of the merry-go-round. Red-and-white-painted wooden horses snorted at lesser attractions and at the candy stands surrounding them.

Our shooting gallery and the ball toss, painted a cheery red and green, flanked the merry-go-round. Opposite, people had already lined up in front of the candy and bratwurst stands. Teenagers and children wandered around in clusters on the trampled grass, looking the attractions over with bright, shiny eyes, their giggles drowned in the brassy music blaring from the merry-go-round's loudspeakers.

"There you are," Vati greeted us as we got out of Carmen's car. "Let's get started." We opened for business, and things were as they had always been, except that Mutti wasn't there. I worked the ball toss, feeling like a carnival attraction myself, shut out from the excitement the local kids my age must have felt and the fun they had with their friends. My sisters ran the shooting gallery across the path.

A voice said, "Hello."

I turned, and my heart grew lighter. Ursula leaned against the ball toss.

I dug change from my pocket and handed it, along with three Ping-Pong balls, to a skinny boy wearing a blue plastic flower in a buttonhole in his shirt. I smiled at Ursula and watched the kid throw the balls. He won a small stuffed bear. I gave it to him, feeling better about my business. I knew how difficult it was to toss such a bouncy little ball into the bowls and have it stay. At least this customer had won something. The boy went away with a happy smile. I saw no new customers and turned to my friend.

"So this is what you do in the summers," Ursula said.

"You mean used to do," I corrected. "I won't be traveling this summer. I'm just helping my Vati when he is close to Wetzlar."

"Can I try one?" Ursula asked.

"Okay. But I can't give you a prize if you win."

I handed her three balls. From the corner of my eye, I noticed someone else familiar. One of the reporters for the *Weztlarer Allgemeine*, the local newspaper, came up to us. The reporter, Brother Uckermann, was a member of the Church. He took his camera from around his neck and snapped a few pictures of me.

"I'll pick the best one to print in the paper," he said. "I'll give you a copy when they are developed."

I nodded. It felt great to see someone who didn't just consider me a carnival kid. I talked with Ursula for a few more minutes, and then her brother called from the candy stand. "I have to go. Are you coming to church tomorrow?"

"Yes, see you there."

"Okay." Ursula smiled and left.

I turned to a small knot of kids ready to try my game.

All day Saturday, I manned the small attraction, listening to the music blaring over the fairgrounds from the merry-go-round. I sold balls to throw and gave away prizes. Mostly I was alone, but sometimes Josefa helped when Vati didn't need her to take tickets at the merry-go-round or help Carmen in the shooting gallery.

Franz also took tickets and made sure the local children sat safely strapped onto their horses, roosters, and other merry-go-round animals before Vati started the ride. I hoped I'd made Vati happy, but the highlight of my day was when my friends from church came to see me and left with a word of encouragement.

That night, in Carmen's car on our way back home, I thought about the next day. It would be Sunday, and I was going to church. I would be back before Carmen was ready to head out to the carnival again.

I rose early the next day and slipped into my pink-flowered dress. Carmen, still in her bed, opened her eyes.

"You're crazy," she said. "Go back to bed." She rolled over and went back to sleep. Josefa, in the bed on the other side, didn't even wake up.

I snuck out and returned in time.

When the spring festival in Finsterloh ended, Vati left on his usual summer circuit, but we girls stayed in our caravan on the Bachweide and went to work every day.

42
ANSWERED PRAYERS

MUTTI PUTS DOWN THE PICTURE OF ME IN THE BALL TOSS. SHE picks up another one. On it, Carmen leans against her Karmann Ghia Volkswagen, a big smile on her face.

"That was a scary time," Mutti says. "I was desperately looking for an apartment I could afford and that was big enough for all of us. Then Carmen made that rash decision. For a time, I wondered if I'd have to give up and get back with your father."

"It was scary for me too."

Mutti doesn't seem to hear me. "For me, it was a little like when I first joined the circus. I worried about what would happen to me."

I thought back to the way I'd felt that summer. Even though I was scared, I was also determined to create my own life, a life away from the carnival, just as Mutti had done.

JUNE 1963

Church was over for the day. Ursula approached me as I left the building.

"Can I come over later? My older sisters will all be at my place. With your sisters gone to the carnival, we can talk and have fun in your small caravan."

I smiled at her. "Sure."

After lunch, I watched out for Ursula. When I saw her walking along the path, I rushed to greet her. We decided to enjoy the sunshine. Talking and laughing, we walked to the place where the rivers Lahn and Dill met and picked tiny wild violets, which grew in profusion along the river-banks in the lovely late-spring weather.

I stood up with a bunch of deep-purple and pink violets in my hand, which contrasted with the paleness of my fist, and looked across the rivers. On the hill in the distance, I made out the Karlsmund, the old ruin left from the time of the Romans. The bright green of the trees surrounded the crumbling tower, and clouds encircled it in a blue sky. How beautiful the world was! With a smile, I turned to Ursula. "These flowers are so pretty, even growing wild. Let's take them home and put them in a glass of water so they won't wilt. When you go home you can take yours with you." I held the flowers to my nose and inhaled the sweet, gentle smell.

We crowded into the larger caravan and rummaged in the kitchen cabinet for two small glasses.

Mutti sat on the sofa, the Sunday paper spread out around her. "Sonja, take Michael and go to the small caravan," she said. "I'm trying to find an apartment, and he keeps messing up the paper."

I scooped up Michael. "Come with us. You can play over there, okay?"

"'Kay," Michael said.

Instead of following me, Ursula put her glass of violets on the kitchen table and turned toward the living room. I stopped.

"I think I heard my mother say something about a large apartment in Giessen," Ursula said. "My older sister is getting married and is looking for a place, but that one was too big for her and her fiancé. Maybe you could go see it."

"That would be great," Mutti said. "Giessen is only ten kilometers from here. And it's bigger than Wetzlar. Do you know the address?"

"No, but I can ask my Mutti and tell you tomorrow."

"How about if Sonja goes home with you later? Can you ask your mother to write it down for me?" Mutti asked.

"Okay," she said.

We went into the small home, where we played with Michael and talked.

At six o'clock, I accompanied Ursula to her home. Her Mutti wrote the address on a slip of paper and gave it to me.

Glad to be useful, I marched home. Halfway across the bridge, a car honked and stopped beside me. Carmen called through the open window, "Come on. I'll take you home."

Josefa, beside her, grinned.

I got into the back. "How is Vati doing?" I asked.

"Fine. He's getting used to working without the rest of the family."

Carmen turned into the small dirt road that led to the Bachweide.

"I have some great news," she said and parked the car next to the caravans.

I followed her into the home, wondering what news would be so great.

Carmen hurried into our large home and found Mutti in the kitchen. I stood by the door, and Josefa crowded next to me.

"I'm going to quit my work at Meier's," Carmen announced.

Mutti looked up from the kitchen counter, where she was cutting bread for supper. Her dark eyes were hard, and a frown shadowed over them. "You can't do that. We need your income to survive. Did your father tell you to do that?"

Carmen leaned against the counter and crossed her arms over her chest. "Vati bought me a small camper trailer, one like the rich people take out for camping in the woods. I want to go with him."

Mutti shook her head. "Then he'd better make sure he pays you enough, so we can live."

I tugged at Carmen's sleeve. "That camper. Is it like the ones the Americans have?" Anything American wildly fascinated me.

Carmen ignored me. "Don't worry about money, Mutti. I'll make more with Vati than I can make at Meier's. I'll make sure you get your money."

"And what will you do in the winters? You won't have an income then."

"That won't be a problem. I'll find something. I work well, and Meier's will give me good references."

"I don't like it. I hoped to keep you all away from the carnival."

"Oh, one more thing." Carmen turned to me. "Sonja, Vati wants you to come next week. He wants you to see my new camper. There'll be two beds, if you want to stay with Vati for the summer too."

I bit my lip. I'd hoped I wouldn't have to go to the carnivals anymore, but I didn't want to disobey or disappoint my father. If he'd ask me right out, I knew I'd say yes, even if it would destroy all hope for my own vision of my future. I said a quick prayer in my heart for God to please help me find a way, without hurting or upsetting my parents, to stay home for good. I hesitated. "I don't think I—"

"Think it over," Carmen interrupted. "In the meantime, he wants you to be there with me next week. We'll leave after work Friday."

"Did you get that address from Ursula's mother?" Mutti interrupted. I handed it to her.

We finished supper. Josefa got out the washbowl. "It's your turn to wash," she said.

"Then you stack the dishes," I countered, grabbing the bowl from her hands. I set it onto the kitchen table, next to the dishes Josefa stacked, and took the water kettle from the hot stove in the living room. It was less than half full, so I went to the water bucket to refill it. The bucket was empty. I straightened and addressed Mutti. "I can't wash the dishes. We're out of water."

Mutti rolled her eyes. "Take the bucket and go get some." She stomped off into the living room, muttering under her breath, "I've had it up to here. I want running water like other people. I want to live in a house again."

I grabbed the bucket, went up the path to the gas station, and filled it from their outdoor faucet.

As I finished washing the dishes, Mutti called from the living room. "Sonja, you stay home from work tomorrow with Michael and Eva. I'm going to take the train to Giessen and see if I can rent that apartment. I'll call your manager from a phone booth."

Mutti left early the next morning. I stayed home and played with Michael, all the while thinking of what Mutti might be doing right then. Maybe the Lord would help her get the apartment, and she would be pleased that someone from church found it for her. Then she would be more tolerant toward me and the Church. *Who knows? Maybe the Lord will soften her heart and she will even join it,* I mused while I took a walk along the riverbanks with Michael. I fed him and Eva when Eva came home from school.

Late in the afternoon, Mutti returned. Her face was dark, and her lips were pressed together. My hopes collapsed. I had been so sure she'd have good news when she returned. Maybe she was upset over something else. "Did you get the apartment?" I asked.

"No. It was big enough, and the rent was reasonable, but they didn't want to rent it to someone with small children."

I couldn't understand it. Hadn't I prayed that she would get that apartment? She even got the information from my church. All my hopes for a more normal life were dashed once again. In the end, I consoled myself. God knew everything. Maybe he wanted to provide an even better apartment for us.

Josefa came home and, a few minutes later, Carmen.

Mutti cut bread for sandwiches. She had bought salami, liverwurst, and Swiss cheese on her way home, and now she put them on the bread slices.

We sat around the table and ate. Carmen asked about the apartment, and Mutti explained she hadn't gotten it.

"I have good news, though," Carmen said. "I gave notice today. Herr Meier said he'd be sorry to see me go, but he said if I wanted to come back after carnival season is over, he'd love to take me back, even if it's only for the winter."

"That's great, child," Mutti said. "That way things will work out just fine, and Vati will have the extra help he needs." She turned to me. "Maybe you can do something like that too, Sonja?"

"Leitz probably won't do such an arrangement. They are a much larger company than Meier's."

"Probably not," Mutti conceded.

Josefa and I took a day of vacation on Friday so we could leave early with Carmen. Carmen drove us to the carnival in Niederbiel, not too far away. Busy with my mixed feelings of seeing Vati again and having to spend the weekend at the carnival, I hadn't noticed Mutti's strange mood that morning.

When we arrived in Niederbiel, I dutifully admired Carmen's new camper home. Josefa and I slept on the seats that converted to a large bed. Like so many times before, Josefa and I worked the ball toss, Carmen ran the shooting gallery, and Franz helped with the merry-go-round.

I was surprised I didn't feel as hopeless about helping Vati as I had a few months ago. As I stood in the ball toss, leaning against the post and waiting for new business, I realized I had a choice. I could either spend my weekends with Vati, just like Carmen, or I could choose to spend them at church and with my member friends, keeping the Sabbath day holy. It was up to me. I had to make my decision and stand by it.

And I chose right there, standing in my ball toss, watching a laughing young man throw another ball, to dedicate my life to Heavenly Father, just as I had promised at my baptism. I decided never again to work in a carnival. Nobody would sway me from that decision.

I closed my eyes and silently prayed that God would help me find a way to make this my last time working at the carnival, without upsetting my parents or embarrassing myself in front of my family.

Sunday night, on the way home, Carmen asked, "So what do you think about my new camper?"

"It's so nice," I said. "You get to live in comfort in the summers, when you are with Vati."

"Why don't you come with me? It would be fun."

"I want to," Josefa said.

Carmen didn't answer. She meant me.

Vati must have told her to invite me, but I didn't feel guilty, as I so often did when I thought of Vati. A deep peace enveloped my soul, and I knew God had granted my wish. Without quite knowing what I would say, I opened my mouth to answer my sister. "You'll be fine by yourself. You'll have your privacy, and you'll get to keep the money without having to share. I'm going to stay in Wetzlar. I need to rest on the weekends to do a good job at work."

"I can go with you if Vati isn't too far," Josefa said. "Then I'll be back early enough on Sundays to rest."

"I'm not going to drive you back and forth all the time," Carmen said to Josefa. She seemed to have forgotten about me. "You'll have to take the train if you really want to come."

"That's fine. It won't be every Sunday, but I'll help out when I can," Josefa said.

We drove the rest of the way in silence. The peace surrounding me when I spoke never left me that night. I knew my life in the traveling carnival was over.

EPILOGUE

WHAT MUTTI DID

I LOOK UP FROM WIPING THE KITCHEN TABLE AND WATCH MUTTI come downstairs from the room she's staying in. She doesn't see the cat on one of the steps and trips over it, but she manages to keep her balance. The cat hisses and streaks off, and Mutti curses under her breath.

I rush from the kitchen, heart pounding. "Are you all right?"

"That darn cat almost made me fall," she says. "I could have broken a bone."

"I'm glad you didn't. The cat usually stays out of people's way. You must have surprised her."

"I still hate cats. They eat birds. Remember little Adolf? Now that was a nice pet."

My heartbeat slows down, and I have to smile. "He sure was. He was always so happy. What made you suddenly decide we needed a new pet in the caravan?"

"I knew we would be getting an apartment soon, and I bought him to celebrate. And with his little black mustache, he looked so much like Hitler, I just had to name him Adolf."

Mutti laughs and I join her. She always had a strange sense of humor, and naming a bird Adolf probably helped her work out the trauma of her life in Nazi Germany.

Mutti gets a faraway look in her eyes. "The day Carmen took you and Josefa to admire her new camper home, I made up my mind. I went to the Wetzlar housing authorities. I hated to do that, but I saw no other way to get us into an apartment."

I pour a cup of coffee for Mutti, get two bowls of cereal, and sit down across from her at the kitchen table. "What happened that day?"

And while Mutti tells me, I see Heavenly Father's guidance in her life, the guidance she still can't see herself.

SUMMER 1963

After Carmen, Josefa, and I left to help with Vati's carnival that Friday, Mutti fed Eva breakfast and sent her to school. Then she dressed Michael and marched with him downtown to the city hall. She pushed open the immense door and found herself in a large foyer dominated by a counter, from behind which a young man with glasses stared at her.

"I want to see the city councilor in charge of housing," she demanded of the receptionist. The young man looked at her as if she were some kind of interesting insect, took her to a small anteroom, and told her to wait.

Mutti sat down, put her purse on her lap, and grasped it tightly. Michael played with his little toy car on the floor.

About half an hour later, the door opened, and a heavyset man with sparse gray hair came in. He introduced himself as Herr Roth and led Mutti and Michael into his office. Mutti found a chair in front of his desk and sat, making sure Michael was comfortable in the large easy chair next to the window.

Herr Roth sat behind his desk, steepled his fingers in front of the clean blotter, and asked, "What can I do for you, *liebe Frau* [dear woman]?"

"We live on the Bachweide, in a caravan," she explained. "I'm divorced and left the carnival. I need an apartment for me and my five children."

"Frau Francesco, surely you are aware of the housing shortage. I can put you on the city waiting list, but it will be at least eighteen months before something will become available." He leaned back in his chair. "Your best bet is to look for something from a private homeowner. There are ads in the paper all the time."

Mutti leaned forward and frowned. "I'm sure you are aware that no one will rent to a single woman with five children. I've been trying to get a place from private parties for the last six months and hear it over and over again. If I had only the older girls, I might have an apartment by now. But no one wants Michael and his eight-year-old sister."

"In that case, I'll put you on the waiting list. You'll just have to take your turn." He smiled. "At least we'll be able to provide you with a large enough apartment eventually, perfect for all your children."

Herr Roth rose and held out his hand.

Mutti stayed in her seat, her arms folded across her chest. She hesitated before deciding to use her last bit of leverage to get out of the caravan with her children as soon as possible. The complacent look in the man's eyes would disappear when she told him, but now she saw no other choice.

"Listen," she said. "I'm half Jewish."

The councilor stared at her. His eyes narrowed. He returned to his seat. "Do you have proof of that?"

Mutti ignored the look of suspicion and defensiveness she saw in his eyes. She told herself this was important. "I have my identification papers, issued during the Third Reich." She dug into her purse and pulled them out. "That should be proof enough. I lost my home and hid in the circus to get away from the Nazis and the concentration camps."

Herr Roth took her papers and rifled through them.

"If you can't get me an apartment," Mutti said, "I will go to the newspaper. I have suffered enough at the hands of German officials, and I'm not willing to suffer anymore." She stood, approached the desk, and leaned against it, giving Herr Roth her disarming, brilliant smile. "I'm sure you'll find a way to put me at the top of your waiting list, and I would be so grateful."

Herr Roth broke eye contact and pulled a ledger from a file next to the desk. He made a notation, closed the ledger, and rose.

"Frau Francesco, this changes things drastically. I had no idea about your true situation. The city government will do what it can to make up for your sufferings. I'll make some phone calls, and you can be assured you'll have an apartment as soon as possible."

Mutti wanted to make sure she wouldn't get the runaround from this man, probably a former Nazi. Still smiling her best, most alluring smile, she asked, "How long do you think I'll have to wait?"

He returned to the ledger and rifled through it. "We're constructing an apartment complex in Albshausen, just six kilometers from here. It isn't finished yet. We're looking at September or possibly October." He closed the book. "That's the earliest we can do, unless you want a much smaller place. Some of the apartments in Albshausen will be quite large, at least three bedrooms."

"One of them will do. Can you give me a written statement, please?"

Herr Roth picked up his pen, wrote a note on a slip of paper, and handed it to her.

Mutti took the paper, rose, and held out her hand. "Thank you so much, councilor. You have been most helpful."

She picked up Michael and left in a hurry before Herr Roth could change his mind. Finally, after all these years of rootless traveling, Michael and the other children would have a real home.

On their way back to the caravan, Michael stopped by the pet store, staring at the puppies and kittens playing in the window. He wouldn't budge, so Mutti went in. A half hour later, she left with a small green parakeet in a brand-new cage.

* * *

On the first of October, 1963, Mutti packed her large suitcase once again. But this time it was for the move. She selected a few of the little children's clothes. Carmen, Josefa, and I chose a couple of outfits we absolutely couldn't do without and piled them into Carmen's car. We left the rest in the boxes the movers would bring. Eva grabbed her favorite doll, and Michael insisted on carrying Adolf in his cage. We all squeezed into the car, and Carmen drove us to our new home. In Albshausen, the car turned into a small, as yet unpaved street. At the end of a brand-new housing development, Mutti pointed out the last apartment building, barely finished and not yet landscaped. Carmen parked in the nearby parking lot, and we catapulted out of the car and followed Mutti to our new home. Mutti opened the door of the building, and we marched after her up the stairway, surrounded by the smells of wood and concrete. We climbed up five stories to the last apartment on the right. Proudly, Mutti took out her new house key and unlocked the door.

The smell of fresh paint greeted us from the open door. Michael, with me right behind him, entered into the spacious place and stopped, still holding Adolf.

I looked around and saw miles and miles of space. The doors to four large rooms stood wide open, and a late-fall sun shone through the uncovered windows. Our few belongings from the caravan, when the movers would bring them this afternoon, would be swallowed up by all the room we had now. I felt free and light.

Michael moved forward, down the hall, and into the largest room. I followed him and thought that he, still so little, would probably never remember much of our life in the carnival. He put down the birdcage and opened its door.

A sunray lit up Adolf's green-and-yellow plumage. He shone like an emerald as he hopped from the cage and soared to the ceiling, so much higher than he was used to in our caravan. I felt as if I could soar with him, high up in this amazing abundance of space, almost close enough to touch heaven, where a loving God watched over me. Out of our cages we would fly and delight in this fine freedom. Like a bird, I was free now to live the life I had always dreamed of.

ABOUT THE AUTHOR

S ONJA HERBERT AND HER FIVE SIBLINGS WERE RAISED IN A caravan, traveling the carnival circuit from town to town in post-World War II Germany.

Sonja converted to the LDS Church, later married, and immigrated to the United States, where she received a bachelor of arts degree at Southern Utah University in Cedar City, Utah, and a master of arts degree from Brigham Young University in Provo, Utah. She also raised six children, taught school and ESL, and is now a freelance writer.

Besides her childhood memoir, Sonja has also written many autobiographical stories, which have been published in the Chicken Soup for the Soul series and other anthologies. A biographical novel about her half-Jewish mother's experiences in Nazi Germany is almost finished.

Sonja lives in Provo with her husband and cat. You can find more about her unusual life at germanwriter.com.